ALMOST THERE

Beauty and Self-Destruction

William J. Milnazik

AuthorHouse™
1663 Liberty Drive
Bloomington, IN 47403
www.authorhouse.com
Phone: 1-800-839-8640

First published by AuthorHouse   12/30/2011

ISBN: 978-1-4685-3910-3 (sc)
ISBN: 978-1-4685-3909-7 (hc)
ISBN: 978-1-4685-3908-0 (ebk)

Library of Congress Control Number: 2012900010

Printed in the United States of America

This book is printed on acid-free paper.

FOREWORD

It would be easy to describe the contents of this book and the process of writing it in colorful and dramatic phrases. Words like "lifelong agony", "the inevitability of a deathly demon", "a brother's loss bleeding out onto the pages" could be used, as well as many other words of a similar and cliché style. They would be appropriate if the goal were to persuade some potential buyer to purchase this book. Sales of almost anything tends to move out of the realm of reality and into the poetic and dramatic. But this is not a novel; it is not a fictitious story springing forth from imagination; it is not a "true story" that holds only seeds of the original reality; it is not a story to be sold. It is a story to be read and acknowledged. It is an accurate delivery of both the events and the emotions of the time. It is the reality of a sister, my sister, who struggled with a disorder for half her life and lost. It is a story of the brilliance of a creative mind and what can happen when the pressures of life and distorted thinking collide. Mostly, it is my observations of a loss and the attempt to understand "why". It wasn't an immediate and sudden loss; it was one that brought with it decades of questions and pain. I haven't used the word "anorexia" prior to this point, because anorexia is one component of the story, but it's an important component. As I travel through the painful events and the irrational and impossible "possibilities" of what might have been, I attempt to create—no, not to create—to deliver the actual events and to reveal my personal thoughts and emotions, and at times, those of my parents. These emotions were a result of being forced to watch a beautiful person suffer with her distorted and destructive thought processes. They were also a result of so many failed attempts to help. There can be a risk when one opens his or her heart and mind; it can open the opportunity for judgment. Readers of this book will certainly have their own opinions of what "should" have been done or what "might" have occurred with a different course of action. Hindsight, especially from a distance is a wonderful luxury. I wish there had been a different conclusion to this story, but we do not have that option, and wishing doesn't change an unfortunate

reality.

I have to write a very strong caveat here. Any medical opinions written throughout this book are just that: opinions. I am a brother not a doctor. To discuss this story and the difficulties that we have experienced, some degree of emotional and medical information has to be discussed. But no specific approach or medical expertise is assumed or even suggested here. Everyone has his or her own path with things like this. These writings are only delivering my experience and my thoughts and opinions.

It's late Thursday,

the day that I first heard that they would have to amputate your legs. I was at work earlier in the day when mom called to let me know what the doctors said. She has always been the strongest emotionally in the family; it's the kind of strength that she never asked for, the kind of strength that comes from a life of care-giving for mothers and uncles and aunts, among others. It's been, at times, a conscious choice and, at other times, a well worn habit. But, that particular moment required more ability than she thought she would ever have to possess. We cried through the call, knowing you probably wouldn't let the doctors take your limbs, and that after this many years of struggle, death would likely be preferable. What is equally sad, or maybe just an odd observation of my own thoughts, is that I almost understand your choice, or at least the choice that I suspect you'll make. After twenty-five years of this slow, unconscious suicide, there is a convoluted logic to letting go… one last time. You have, after all, been letting go of life piece by piece, unconsciously, for years—or maybe it has been with more thought than we know—deliberately shutting down life in carefully measured and calculated portions.

Kim, you are my sister. We were born of the same parents. We spent our youth together as most siblings do. We took family vacations together, exploring the crystal waters of the Caribbean or learning to water ski in the mountains of Pennsylvania. We ran downstairs together to discover what Santa Claus had left for us under the Christmas tree. We navigated the trials of adolescence and college—differently, but together. I have always admired your talent and your kindness, but for half of my life, you haven't been there. In your place was an almost nonexistent body and a mind, a brilliant mind, but one that was getting buried deeper and deeper in its own desire for perfection. It can be so easy to abandon everything in search of a successful career. I have watched myself at times fall into that same trap, but to a lesser degree. Like any machine, like any functioning device, a career needs to produce something in order to justify its existence, otherwise it becomes little more than a hobby or pastime. You demanded such perfection of yourself that no finished product could ever come off the end of your production line. As time passed with this illness, less and less was "good enough". Perfection had become your enemy, your addiction, your assassin. Yet, with a tight grasp, you held it close and protected it from the few remaining people that have been trying to help you through this for half (the last half) of your life.

Our family has come to understand the word "anorexia" better than most, or at least the complex version of it that you have held onto so tightly. We've experienced it in ways that can splinter a family and empty one's heart of hope. The effects of an illness like this go so far beyond any single person. Kim, you are foolish to think that you can be an island, separating yourself from the world around you. Your actions do have effects on others. We aren't experts, as if there are actual experts on something this complex, and we don't have a great deal of clinical knowledge about this disease. I, too, have watched the TV specials and listened to the news stories. Each time I recognized a familiarity but tried to hold on to or maybe cling to the thought that our situation "isn't that bad." Maybe things could change if we could only work with the problem... if you would only work with the problem... if you would only

let us

Self-destructive behavior in a family member brings with it fear, hope, denial, work, pain, and ultimately what I now see for us: failure. As I write this, sitting on my sofa, you, my sister, are in the intensive care unit of Paoli Hospital. Your body is malnourished to the point that the circulation in your legs has almost completely shut down. A body does that in order to protect the organs... in order to protect... life. It's the biological equivalent of military troops retreating behind a smaller and smaller area for protection. Your white blood cell count and glucose levels are way off and you are not responding to normal treatment. Gangrene is beginning to set in on your blue, purple, and black legs. I am waiting for the phone call that will tell me to come to the hospital and say goodbye. All of this because of your own choices. A child should never die before her parents... especially at her own hands.

in!

I feel guilt about the thought of accepting your death. My mind struggles to prepare my heart for the inevitable, but is this abandoning hope? The doctors say that there is a slight chance that the nourishment they are flowing into your veins might be enough to save your life… and maybe, if we are extremely lucky, even your legs. But they also say that you are too weak to undergo any surgery right now, and even if they do amputate, you may not have the strength to survive. Is this medical nourishment a morbid version of fattening the calf for slaughter? Getting you to the point where you are strong enough to have your legs amputated?

My mind searches everywhere for logic or reason.

This point in time is the result of a combination—your combination—of compulsive behavior and anorexia. It comes at the end of countless conversations and decades of emotions ranging from hope, optimism and sympathy to anger, guilt, and sadness. It comes at the end of so many doctors making so many diagnoses. It comes at the end of so many years of your brilliant and conscious (or possibly subconscious) manipulation of us to keep us at a distance. We are now, without the help of a miracle, losing half of the children in our already small family. For many years, I have felt alone without a sister, but I'm now beginning to feel the intensity of a mixture of emotion that wraps together fear, hurt, anger, and some other emotions that are completely unfamiliar to me. And I have no choice but to feel them all.

ANOTHER STEP... BACKWARDS

Three weeks ago—in my day-to-day obsessions about business, sales, schedules, and the daily questions of, "Am I doing my best work?"—I picked up the phone. On the other end I heard Mom's voice say, "Your sister has fallen and broken her hip." At the age of fifty, a broken hip sounded a little odd... unless we were to consider your physical condition. After getting you to the hospital, mom, dad and I talked, knowing what a broken hip could mean to an elderly person and considering your diminished health. It was later that day, when I was visiting you in the hospital, that I learned that you had literally fallen asleep standing up while working on plans for a stained glass window. No doubt a result of no more than three hours sleep for many consecutive nights and the bare minimum of food intake for months. The previous twenty-five years had not been much different, but you had been pushing yourself even harder in recent weeks. The doctor said that you had the brittle bones of an eighty-year-old woman and your hip had just snapped when your exhausted body hit the cement basement floor.

In a medically mechanical process, they opened your hip and attached a plate and screws so that the bone could heal—a relatively common surgery. I sometimes wonder what the conversations, or at least the thoughts, were around the operating table—seeing the emaciated body of an anorexic woman, with the expectation that they were supposed to "fix" it. It was clear to us, and I have no

Night Wind

What the heart believes is never lost
Though sometimes to give it up seems the
Relief for which we would be most grateful.
And as time passes by one belief or
Another, and still another, and the
Pain of the loss intensifies, then
Diminishes, the sense that there is
Something more arrives from the stillness
That centers the suffering as it
Recasts identity. And somewhere
The seeds from the dead flowers have been
Cradled on the wind as we can feel
Without knowing, and that awareness is
Followed through even across the open
Car that passes by, and its music that
Extends far beyond in the way of
Aspirations of which no one
May yet be aware.

Bill R.

doubt that it was clear to the doctors and nurses as well, that fixing a hip would not fix a broken life. It was like patching a hole in a tire when all the remaining rubber was all but rotted out. Surgical actions in a case like this seem to be more about giving hope than giving health, and for so many years, you had been slowly but continually stripping us of that hope, while you were draining the life from your own body. After all the talk, all the family discussions, and the years of occasional therapy, we thought that maybe, just maybe, this event could have been the reality check that would have finally enabled you to see what you were doing to yourself. It's amazing how one always reaches for a glimmer of optimism no matter how often or severe the disappointment. Human nature is wonderfully and at times foolishly resilient that way.

I returned to my frustration and sadness when I visited you in the hospital and listened to you casually talk as though this had been just an accident, a minor inconvenience. There wasn't a glimmer of understanding or acknowledgement of the severity of the event. You had once again perfected the skill of denial. It was a few days later when clarity began to creep into your mind. Maybe it was the fear of death or the understanding that this was not the way to live a life. We heard you hint, for the first time ever, about your mistakes and that you wanted to learn how to be healthy. This may not sound like much to most people, but after twenty-five years of firm and almost complete disregard of our help with a very polite, "Thank you, but you're wrong, and besides, I don't have time to talk to a therapist, or to see a doctor," any admission of a problem was miraculous. We even heard through alternate channels that you had been talking to a social worker about going to an eating disorder center, something we had discussed with you numerous times. *Maybe, just maybe,* we were turning a corner here, being heard, making a difference.

In addition to your surprising shift in thinking, we were also working, outside of your awareness, to make a change. When we knew of only a broken hip, we decided that, with your history, a history that we knew all too well, this was far too serious to leave the decision-making up to you alone. But you were an adult, so we also knew that we had a very thin legal foundation to stand on. We (Mom, Dad and I) were getting together with a therapist that Mom had already been seeing in order to work around some of the absolute insanity of HIPPA regulations and to do what was needed to try to save your life. It was this therapist, in discussions with another therapist whom we had all but forced you to see, that first discussed the existence of an obsessive-compulsive component to your already difficult situation. Whether it was a moment of confusion or possibly a moment of clarity, it didn't matter. You gave us the "okay" to talk with your therapist. I wonder now if your decision was from a newly found understanding of your own mortality or simply from the exhaustion of surgery and rehabilitation. Finally, for the first time ever, after twenty-five years of attempting to help you out of this self-destruction, we had the opportunity to bring all parties together and discuss openly how we could help. We discussed an intervention of sorts that would leave you no choice but to enter an eating disorder clinic. But we also knew that, as an adult, you had the right to check yourself out at any time, or even to refuse to go at all. We made the best plans we could, uplifted by the interest that you showed in accepting help and by your sudden acknowledgement of a struggle that we had been watching for so many years. It was a realization that came from a discussion you had with a social worker. After all of our attempts to show you what you were doing to yourself, it was someone outside of our family that had finally gotten you to see the truth. I am so grateful to her for making that effort and for sharing what she heard with us. This raised our hopes enough to actually risk thinking about a real solution for the first time in so many years. It had always been simple; we would see the truth and the self-destruction and we would ask and plead and discuss all the realities of malnutrition, habitual behavior, and self-sabotaging actions. Yet unless you were to agree to lower your self-protection and think, even for a moment, that you might be making some very serious and life-threatening decisions, we could do nothing. This disorder has a complex ability to ensure its own survival. Because of malnutrition, a pattern of distorted thinking is seen as truth and reality. That "perceived" truth encourages more malnutrition, creating more distorted thinking, causing a life-threatening (or ending) spiral.

How did we know that you had agreed to go to an eating disorder clinic? It wasn't from your words. For the moment, we had a spy.

The HIPPA regulations have a way of preventing everyone from hearing about one's personal health. In this case, even family members were prevented from hearing anything from anyone… other than you. HIPPA is a very convenient wall that the mentally ill can hide behind. It's a constructed barrier that separates those that need help from the very people, and at times the only people that care enough, know the person well enough and are in a position to help. To be fair, there are many cases in which privacy is an important aspect, especially in this age when corporations love little more than profiting from the details of one's personal information. But it also prevented us from knowing the truth, or at least having the factual, professional diagnosis that could have shown us the severity of the situation before it was too late.

A social worker was "leaking" information about you to Mom. I don't know her name and have never met her, but I will be eternally grateful that there was one person amongst years of therapists and doctors that understood the importance of honest and open communication and the damage that can occur from the rigid misuse of regulations. With an illness like this, or any other involving self-destructive behavior, knowing the truth is critical. The social worker was a connection to your real thoughts and real situation. We were able to plan and work on the "outside" and adjust to what was really going on, not to what you were so carefully allowing us to think. In this case, now, finally, we were given the knowledge that you understood the truth… after twenty-five years… and that knowledge was invaluable. It gave us, even if only for a short time, the ability to work *with* you on this, not as adversaries. And maybe most importantly for us, it gave us the hope that there just might be a happy and healthy future for you.

A TURN FOR...

It couldn't have been written much better. Endless Hollywood movies use this same blueprint in order to create drama and shift the emotions of moviegoers. Wave an element of hope in front of them just before crushing them with the sorrow of inevitability.

Months before your fall, you had developed an infection on your ankle that would not heal. It grew deeper and more severe, almost reaching the bone. This was another result of your illness. The human body can only do so much with a lack of sleep and nourishment over that long a period of time. You had talked of the pain from the infection so I knew it was severe because you rarely complained about anything. I had the arrogance to take it lightly, in the privacy of my own mind almost blaming you for causing it. In the hospital, the doctors became more concerned with the infection than the postoperative care for your broken hip. A choice had to be made. In your compromised state, the antibiotics, the powerful ones needed for this infection, would also kill much of the protective bacteria that your body required, running the risk of lowering your already compromised self-defense system. Yet the infection was getting more serious and needed attention. You and Mom weighed out the pros and cons of different approaches and decided to proceed with the antibiotic. It did its job. It killed everything... everything except for the one bacterium in your intestine that your body was already barely keeping in balance. That bacterium now had a chance to grow without the check and balance of your body's normal healthy defense. When an average person is afflicted with vomiting and diarrhea from this type of illness, the pain and discomfort are considerable, and it can be very serious, but it isn't normally something that guarantees death. For you, the physiology was very different. You had taken your body and health right to the edge over so many years of slow and unconsciously methodical starvation. Your body was at the point where any stress would push you past your ability to fight. You simply had no more reserves to draw upon. There was nothing left. The skeleton of a human form that I so often looked at with heartache had lost the ability to do what is so fundamentally human... survive. When I step back and look at the years of struggle that led to your death, I sometimes wonder if you hadn't died years before and your body was just now catching up.

I think what makes me the saddest, and yet what still gives me a sliver of odd but honest contentment (we are past the time for hope now) is that we had a glimpse at an end to this, an end that involved your admission to the problem. Few personal problems are ever solved without an admission early on in the process. And for the first time in many years, we were given one. In addition to this glimpse, we saw a point where we might have been invited in to help rather than being rejected as we had been for twenty-five years. I love you, my sister, and I have gone through times when I almost gave up, every time coming back to try something else, to discuss it differently, and to try again. The break of privacy from the social worker suggested that you understood,

...your body was now merely catching up.

that you had seen the real problem and that you could have asked us for help. It was a gift of great value to us. And now, when we live with the pain of knowing that those thoughts arrived too late to save your life, they still hold some awkward comfort, knowing that you were able to finally understand, that you were capable of seeing the truth. The other aspect that rips at my heart is that you were in the midst of an internal struggle that must have been making your life a seemingly impossible uphill task, needing to grasp onto some solid truth yet not seeing the result of your intense struggle and hard work. Even through endless offers of help and questions, you kept it to yourself. Or, maybe you really just didn't know that life could be different. We, as a human species, do tend to live right up to our own visions of ourselves in the world without seeing the possibilities that lie just on the other side of our self-constructed limitations. But I find it hard to believe, with all the help and observations that we offered, the discussions and the therapy that we first suggested and at times almost forced on you, that there was rarely a hint of acknowledgement. I wonder, in your times of quietly listening to us, with your replies of hearing and understanding, if you were simply agreeing to the therapy to placate us, never really believing or investing in anything that was said. Was it simply another way to keep us at a distance… to buy more time? And at this point I have to now ask, time for what?

Tough love is a difficult thing. When somebody is hurting herself, we like to give her the choice to make the right decision. We coach, we talk, we help, and we desperately want her to make healthy choices. We believed that, if you made the right choices out of a real understanding, a solution was much more likely than if we were to force you to do anything that you were not truly invested in. Anorexia, at least this version of it, seemed to be so much like alcoholism or drug abuse. There was a blindness that came with the illness… a complete inability to see the reality. Should we have pushed harder? Should we have taken a different approach? It was too late to think about all the "shoulds" and "might have beens". You were lying in a hospital bed, depleted of any ability to fight this; you were dying.

A CREATIVE PRISON

It was about eight years ago when your career as an illustrator suffered to the point that you needed to move out of your apartment and into Mom and Dad's house. I can look at it as a commentary on their love for you that they took you in, but I suspect that they viewed it as simply taking care of their child, without any thoughts of emotional measurements. I'm sure that at age forty-two, it was a difficult move and a painful admission of a suffering career. Yet that was another point of optimism for us. We thought that, with regular contact with people and the ability for us to be there to help, we could help you turn around, or more accurately, turn your disease around. It was not to be. Over the years, you became more and more of a recluse, spending less and less time with the few people that you still allowed into your life.

Years earlier, in what I now look back on as the first major indication of a problem, you severed relationships with your friends, and for about a year, you chose not to communicate with us as well, and you continued to live in the perfection you so demanded of yourself. In some ways, it was a sort of self-fulfilling prophecy. Your philosophy was a simple one and in the hands of a healthy person, it would have been a valid and often respected philosophy: "When confronted with a problem, work harder to solve it." You were unable to see that the problem was not your talent; it was not your creativity; it was not your ability as an artist. It was your endless answer, your single view that more perfection was needed and the inability to see the real problem: your own thoughts.

All of us in the family have worked in the creative fields. Our father was a graphic designer. (At the time the career was called "commercial artist".) Mom was a fashion illustrator. They are both extremely talented painters now. After 17 years working for a design firm, I have followed my father's path and opened my own graphic design and marketing business. We all know the creative drive and the struggle of applying it to a business. One of the difficulties with the artistic creative process is that there is no end to it. Unlike math, or many of the sciences, there is no completion once the "right" answer is found. There is always another viewpoint; more research or fine-tuning that can be done. In any creative business, it's an interesting question, when to release work and when to work further on one's own view of perfection. You were an extremely talented artist, but the "perfect storm" for you joined forces here. Two seemingly unrelated elements—your illness and your career as an artist—worked as two lenses, each magnifying the other. I don't want to say that art caused your problems. You came into this world with a predisposition towards perfection. At a young age you were the one dutifully working on detailed paintings while I was out playing in the woods. In later years, as we were both working hard at our college careers, I also took some time off to sneak a case of beer for me and some buddies or to go away with my girlfriend on a vacation now and then. For you, perfection was simply a way of life. It got you respect both in school and in an early career, and I have to say, even now after your death, your work, the work that you allowed yourself to complete, is beautiful and admired by so many. However, when the time spent on any business endeavor exceeds the budget, when the creative process no longer functions as a viable business, what does one do? The only skill you knew was to strive harder for perfection and to try to increase the demand for your work through making work that only you could create. An admirable philosophy here, but there was a trap. The more trouble you had managing the time needed for

May 2006

In my art teaching career of 35 years, there have been thousands of students, most of them long gone, never to be seen again. A select few possessed the skills and character that placed them on a short list of unforgettable artists and appealing personalities. Kim was certainly among them – very talented, quite personable, and endowed with an increasingly rare quality in young people: a strong work ethic. We would discuss an art process one day, and by the next day that step would be completed. She was a student who made me proud to be a teacher, and I have always had fond memories of Kim.

We recently reconnected at one of Bill's parties, and I was looking forward to more interaction and discussion with a serious artist and friend. Much to my chagrin, this will never be. I believe artists each have demons to face, and we do what we can to achieve peace and balance in our lives. It is sad to note that the life of such a special person was cut short – I can only hope that Kim has found her peace.

21

projects, the more you felt like a failure. (Your words, not mine.) That feeling resulted in your demand for your own perfection so you could gain the career acknowledgement and the level of work that could justify the time you "needed" to spend. This resulted in projects not being completed simply because they were never "good enough". This, in turn, created more of a feeling of failure in your mind. It was an ever-tightening, self-perpetuating circle of distorted logic. Your solution: work harder. Each step further involved less sleep and less nourishment. I don't completely understand the nourishment aspect other than to say that there was a tighter and tighter desire to control your life, and less self-worth, which may have taken the form in your mind as, "I don't deserve much," or, "I don't have time for eating." Extreme calculations were made about time allotments, calories, and just about every aspect in your life. Your writing got smaller and smaller. You filled endless papers with thoughts, plans, and ideas about everything from where to get better visual reference for a plant in a minute section of a painting, to legal advice, to supply resources, to the calories of various food supplements and how they could replace real food. And all these calculations, ideas, thoughts, and misdirected plans became your sole focus. We were forced into a position of sifting through what you would tell us, separating the damaging, self-destructive thoughts from the creative ones that might help your career. We saw some of these ideas as both your "heart's desires" and possible solutions and wanted to support them. At the same time, they were all, in one way or another, aspects of the illness that took your life.

When you moved back into the house that we grew up in, you needed a studio space to do your work. The basement was the obvious choice. It had plenty of space and good northern lighting, atypical of a normal basement. You quickly spread out to fill it with notes, sketches, research material, books, paints, and a variety of other tools and materials. I always love seeing places like metal shops, artist's studios, auto shops; the places where work is done. There is a sense of energy, or maybe it's a personal soul that seems to reside where manual work is performed. I felt it here, too, but for the first time, I was seeing it as part of a bigger problem. As your passion became more obsessive, we watched you retreat further and further into your work, caring less and less about anything else. You began to take on the appearance of the homeless women that I regularly saw in the years of walking to work at a design studio in Philadelphia. Your eyes sunken back in your head, your feet began to take on a bright magenta color from lack of circulation, and through your constant soft-spoken kindness, I began to notice a hesitation or slowness in your thoughts and speech. Your studio began to look like the scene from the movie *A Beautiful Mind* in which they discover the building behind the house covered with notes and scribbles, all extremely deliberate, yet missing an element of functionality. With the goal of sleeping less and working more, you began to spend greater and greater amounts of time near your work. For you, the basement became not only a place to work, but a place to live. You had a clean and comfortable bed in your childhood bedroom upstairs but you chose a sleeping bag on the basement floor. It was a tactic to avoid any wasted time sleeping. You were sinking. And all the logic and help in the world could not change your destructive thought process.

"Why didn't we do something?"

"Why didn't we take you to a doctor or force you to eat?" We will ask ourselves these questions and many more for the rest of our lives. But this opens the door to aspects of personalities, the medical system, and the intense and almost brilliant ability of a self-destructive person to keep people at a distance. As time passed, we began to realize that things were not changing for the better. With my limited medical knowledge, I knew that anorexia was largely based on control issues. Food was a by-product of the problem, not the problem itself, although, it could easily perpetuate the problem in the hands of one with distorted thinking. We began to talk more directly with you about what you were doing, how to find help, whom to turn to.

To do anything that took time away from your work was just unthinkable for you. At our request, we started having regular family meetings, because you had perfected the ability to manipulate a conversation when it was one-on-one. It was odd. In these meetings you would quietly listen. It hurt so much to deliver our direct and honest opinions of what you were doing to yourself. The pain however, of hurting you with the truth began to fade compared to the pain of letting your spiral continue. During these meetings, you sort of fell on the sword of your own shame and, by your definition, your own failure. We tried so hard to follow a very simple and basic rule: Praise what was good and discuss openly the areas that were causing problems, each time giving suggestions as to other, more productive options. In retrospect, I know you felt real shame, but I wonder if you didn't use this tactic of self-condemnation to keep us at a distance from both you and your illness. How can one firmly treat a person that is crushed down to the slightest shell of emotional and physical existence? You would then quietly but firmly request more time to complete the latest project. Your work was your reason for being, your soul, and we thought that if you were able to succeed at one of your own creations—with our support and direction—you might be able to change the destructive patterns of your life. This became an endless and repeated experience. I can think of at least ten different projects, some taking over two years. Every one of them resulted in sketches, beautiful sketches that would have been the seeds of incredible work. Some were amazing pieces of art in themselves. Yet none of the work was ever ready for you to release. None of it could pass the ever-increasing rigidity of your own criteria. In our discussions, there was a very soft but very rigid stubbornness about you. Was it conscious or unconscious manipulation? Simply your personality? Probably all three.

We did step up—for lack of a better term—the "management" of your problem. There was no choice. This task fell mostly on Mom and Dad, since you now lived with them and they could be there with subtle comments or stronger and direct discussions. I tried to be available and initiate conversation when I could. I remember vividly, at one point, we were in a family meeting, during which I was making a suggestion, and you blurted back to me in a very rare moment of anger, "You don't know what I've been doing. You're not here!" It was an attempt to invalidate my comments. I remember feeling both the admiration and appreciation of your strength and determination as well as a sadness knowing that your defenses and the self-protection of the illness were stronger than I thought. It was an open and honest delivery of how you felt, and it showed how rigidly you were attached to your one solution. I said, "You're right, but I talk with Mom and Dad about what is going on and can see the self destructive pattern of your behavior. Besides, if you can show me how your philosophy is resulting in success, I will happily back off in my suggestions." It was at that point that I began to think that my periodic visits and discussions were not enough. Mom, who has an endless concern and care for people, sometimes at her own detriment, was becoming the pivotal point in this. A woman who, at the age of twelve, began taking care of her own mother when her father died of lung cancer and who, as an only child, in later years stepped in to take care of both of our grandmothers and many of our grandmother's sisters as they aged. Mom, whether she wanted it or not, had spent much of her life in the role of caregiver. But Kim, you required skills that were unknown to Mom and to the rest of us. I suspect in the years to come, we will spend quite a bit of time trying to accept that we simply didn't have the skills we needed. I have to believe that the correct combination of knowledge and actions exists somewhere. Otherwise, the only thought left is that your life and death were simply your destiny with no other possible ending. Was it our destiny then to try to help and fail and eventually just witness the end of your life?

Friday, March 3, 2006, 10:32 a.m. We watched the hospital monitor as the distance between each breath and each heartbeat grew in length. We sat with you for about an hour and a half, alternately holding your hand and whispering in your ear that it was alright, that we loved you, and that you could let go. When someone is dying, when there is no room left for hope, there seems to be this desire to know the unknowable and to pretend as if we know what is best. Maybe it was a selfish statement with the real goal of stopping *our* pain, but we said, "It's okay; you can let go now," like we not only knew what you were experiencing but that we knew what you "should" have been doing. Or, maybe, it was an assumption that, even in death, you would still try to be considerate of us and try to hold on. "Don't worry about us; just let yourself go." It sounds so stupid now.

We had received a call from the hospital at 8:25 a.m. You were dying. I was on the way to work, and got a call from Mom. As I turned my car in the direction of their house to pick them up, my life began to change. It wasn't like I hadn't thought about this many times before. I thought I was prepared for your death. I wished for a different outcome, but I honestly thought I would be okay if or when you died from this. After years of this struggle, I couldn't help but prepare myself for it. But one *can't* truly prepare for this. The drive to the hospital was quiet with the attempt to understand that this was the end. It was quiet with the struggle to grasp the truth that you were leaving us, that the years of discussions, advice, support, and medical attention had failed. It was quiet as we absorbed one fact: You were dying.

When we arrived at the hospital, the nurse met us. From what I can remember, she was pleasant, dark-haired, maybe thirty-ish… although, all this could be completely wrong, blurred through the lens of the emotional pain. She said that you had asked her if you were dying. She said that she had told you "Yes," and that you had quietly said, "Okay." Until that point, we hadn't known if you were conscious or not, if we were just going to sit with your body until your life slowly drained out or if we would have the chance to "see" you, to talk with you. We pulled the curtain back; you looked up and said hello to each of us with a quiet and slow but deliberate voice. The painkillers and the complete shut down of your body had taken away any fine points of your speech. You were too tired to put together more than a few words at a time. But you were there, and so were we… to share in the end of your life

The limited conversation was mixed between tears and statements of love and your simple observations about your final experiences. "The blanket is too heavy," or in a moment of quiet, when we were just watching you, in a softly broken speech: "Step back… nobody likes… to be stared at." Yet, when someone you love is only going to be with you on this earth for minutes, there is an uncontrollable desire to look at them. It may be a need to share what little time is left, to communicate the impossible through the connection of the eyes. Maybe it's the desire to actually believe that we can see when the soul leaves the body. Either way, we watched, but were a little less obvious because of your request.

When the doctor pulled Mom and Dad out of the room, I stood over your bed with no attempt to hold back the tears. I said that we needed to say goodbye and that I loved you. You looked at me and asked, "Am I dying?" Although I did my best not to show it, I froze, wondering what to say. I assumed that either the drugs or just the condition of your body had allowed you to forget what the nurse had previously said. The initial question of, "Should I be the one to tell you?" crossed my mind. If so, how should I tell a dying person that all that she had struggled for, all that she had been hoping for, all that she wanted to be for herself or for others would be over in hours… or maybe minutes? I grasped at the thought that honesty was all I could offer. Like many people, we sometimes try to sugar coat issues, not out of deception but out of a desire not to hurt or condemn someone else. Now was not the time for that. "It looks that way" I said, "but there is always room for miracles." Even then, in some dark corner of my mind, I still had to hold onto the possibility of some other ending to this. Was this little piece of hope for you or for me? I don't know. You kind of acknowledged it with a short moment of consideration and a small nod. Through my tears, I said, "I'm going to miss you." You looked up with your blue eyes, still strikingly bright, although your skin had taken on many different colors that skin had no business being. You said, "I'm going to miss you, too."

In a short while, you seemed to get tired and asked for something to ease the pain. We were surprised when, in your severely weakened state, you were able to do something as simple as swallowing a Percocet. The nurse offered morphine, but you said that morphine hurt. It seemed odd to me, that in your final moments, when the functions of your body were shutting down, you were able to determine the subtleties of one pain killer versus another, or that something as strong as morphine could be associated with pain. The nurse eventually came back with something else—Demerol maybe—and said that this would make you relax and help you to breathe more easily. I have no way of knowing, but from this experience and from being by our grandmother's side as she died in the hospital, it seems that in moments like these, when it clearly becomes only a matter of time, hospitals have this unspoken way that they allow the person to slip painlessly into death. I suppose that some right to life group or some zealot about God being the only one to take a life could be inclined to create a picket line in front of any hospital or petition the government to step in. But personally, I thank God, the supreme being, or whatever name you want to use, that with our infinite drive to develop technology to the point where we can keep a body alive almost indefinitely, we still have some people that know the difference between a life and a physical body and are able to make the tough choices and don't hide behind some brainwashed, black and white belief system.

Kim, your conversation had all but stopped at this point. We sat with you as the signals of consciousness left one by one. Your eyes drifted back in your head, your mouth fell open, and a grey cast slowly washed across your face. We sat for about an hour and a half, holding your hands, stroking your hair… and looking. You could no longer be annoyed by our stares. We needed to get a glimpse of that soul, if just for a split second as it left your body to say, "We love you." We needed to see the Kim that we always knew was inside as you passed in front of us and into the ether. Or maybe it was somehow to see that you were okay and that the pain of this life was over. Our mother is more religious than Dad and I, but I think we all agreed that there was a solemn correctness about being there with you, and for you at your passing. It was both a surreal and an extremely real experience watching the monitor for the technical signs of death and balancing that with just being with you. As I now think back on the actual visual image of your death, it was the saddest and most pathetic thing I have ever seen. "Pathetic" is a word often used in condemnation of someone or some thing, but in this case "extremely sad" is a more accurate definition. The infection had reduced your body to the smallest remnant of a human form, maybe ninety-five pounds (at a height of five-foot-seven-inches). Your eyes were sunken way back in her head; there was not a muscle or ounce of fat to pad the skin over your bones. Before Mom pulled the blanket over your foot in a polite and caring gesture, I noticed the deep purples and blacks in your skin, the beginning stages of gangrene. Your hands had started to turn purple on your fingertips, but changed to more of a yellow cast as you passed into death. All of this was something you might have accepted in a ninety-five-year-old person that was passing from life, yet you laid there at age fifty with the visual youth of your still naturally dark brown hair. How you managed to avoid graying hair with all the other physical damage you accepted is beyond me. The image just didn't make sense.

After about a half hour, the readout indicating your breathing slowed to the slightest blip… and then nothing. A straight green line with the word "arrhythmia" below it. Your heartbeat continued for another fifteen minutes, slowly extending the distance between each spike. The mountains turned to hills, the valleys changed into plains, slowly becoming another straight green line. I wondered how little oxygen and how small of a heartbeat could keep a body alive. We waited. We held your hands, and we watched.

Then you were "gone."

"gone"

The nurse came in and disconnected the monitor. What tears were left came flooding out quickly. In a moment when intense emotions seemed to be the most appropriate, the whole scene oddly shifted to the practical aspects of, "What do we do now?" Maybe it was a natural desire to hurt less, substituting the pain for the task at hand. In front of you, we discussed what to do with your body. The discussion seemed uncomfortable to me, but decisions had to be made. The hospital suggested an autopsy to determine why the intestinal bacteria had spread so quickly. Years before, you had made the request to donate your organs upon death. How were we to do that? What did we have to sign? I attempted to make a few phone calls, some personal and a couple just trying to handle a few urgent aspects of self-employment. I had to cancel a meeting that was scheduled for later that day. I thought that I could keep it together long enough to deal with the call.

I was wrong.

I lost my ability to separate personal emotion from business. In an attempt to control my pain long enough to explain why I could not make it to the meeting, I quickly found myself in a mix of broken speech and tears.

Apparently, if an autopsy is done, the body is no longer useful for donating organs. We tried to protect your wish but soon found out that, with the infection and your diminished physical condition, your organs were not wanted. Even after your death, your illness was preventing you from being what you wanted to be in this world. This was yet another point of sad irony. We then chose to let the hospital do the autopsy. It was our second-to-last attempt to create at least some benefit for you after your death. If a doctor could use this information to save a single person in the future, it would be worth this decision.

There is a point when the desire not to accept a death turns one's thinking to blame. I wondered why a doctor would knowingly give you this antibiotic when a possible, and in your case likely, result could be the explosion of this intestinal bacteria, especially in your physically devastated state. Maybe this was where other people call their lawyer and look to some monetary injection to ease their pain. It could have been a mistake. It could have been a calculated risk that failed. It could have been the only solution with the bone infection. The truth is that you had made choices in your life that resulted in this. You had lived at such a minimal level that you could not survive what a healthy person might have. And all the lawsuits and financial reimbursement in the world would not ease the pain of your loss or bring you back into our lives.

Dear Janet and Bob,

I especially remember last summer—
I saw Kim come down the hill to say
Hello to me—Told her how happy to
see her again especially now—as there were
about 3 toddlers playing with the chalk on
the driveway. Kim—drew pictures for them
Boats—beautiful—large—Boats in the
water. The toddlers—were quiet and
watched. I took a picture of Kim—still have
it.

I remember Kim as a toddler going up to
visit Alma and get her cookie—one to eat—
one in her pocket. Alma always had them
ready. Janet called ahead—to be sure. We all
watch carefully until Kim arrived home.
The hill—is steep for a toddler

NEWS

As we drove home, each of us, in our own way, tried to grasp the reality that you were gone. I don't know if it's better or even possible to accept it all at once. It seems to sometimes seep in with strong waves and at other times with long periods of low-grade ache. And this is only the beginning of the mourning, the grieving, and the attempt to understand "why".

We got back to Mom and Dad's house and walked through the front door to a house where, after years of hearing or just knowing that there was activity and life aside from Mom and Dad, we now saw it as empty. We silently walked inside, stopped, and looked at each other as if to say, "Now what?"

The next stage that seems to take place is the obligatory delivery of this news to the closest family and friends. It's partially because they deserve to know and partially because there is a need to let others know that we are in paralyzing emotional pain. We need their help. I guess this, too, will be an evolution through the close family and friends to the "secondary" acquaintances, and then to the point where I will be at a store and run into a person from years past who asks, "How's your sister?" The early and middle stages seem to help with this path, but I'm not looking forward to the time at the store when, while in the middle of some mindless shopping experience, I am immediately pulled back to the memory of this emotion.

A few years earlier, Susan (our second cousin) and her husband Sanj had moved into the house next door. It had been her father's house and one where, as children, you and I would run down the hill and watch Aunt Ethel (Susan's mom) work at her pottery wheel or we would play on their swing set. Susan and Sanj have been the best neighbors I could possibly wish for our parents. They manage that wonderful balance of being supportive as well as just being fun people. When we arrived home, I felt the need to do something, anything, yet there was nothing that would change the pain I felt. Needless to say, Susan and Sanj needed to know. I walked down the hill and delivered the news. We just cried for a while. Sajel (their three-year-old daughter) kept asking, "Why are you sad, Mommy?" Susan answered, "There was a very special person that didn't know how wonderful she was." You would from time to time stop your work long enough to walk next door and enjoy the company of a child, using her oversized chalk to draw something playful on the driveway, sharing stories, or helping her play dress-up.

Soon, all of us (Mom, Dad, Susan, Sanj, Chanin [my fiancée] and I) were at the house just talking, crying, trying to understand, and trying to ease the pain. The conversation, as I suspect commonly does in time of death, turned to history and memories of youth. In this case the topics were your talent, your stubborn drive for perfection, and simple little life stories like the sadness of seeing the now forty-six-year-old orange tree that you had planted when you were four. In your youth, it held only the naive optimism of planting a seed. Now it suddenly represented pain, death, and loss. For me, there was a need to discuss the past few hours. I don't know why, but I no longer felt the desire to protect you by delivering minimal news. Or maybe finally, it was the feeling that I had the right to talk about what I felt and to share the pain in the hope of diminishing it, even just the smallest amount. Is emotional pain something that can be diluted by sharing it with others?

Phone calls came and phone calls went. There was a need to put the news out, because not only were there people that cared about you and deserved to hear about your death, but also because you deserved to have this information delivered. Your life had ended. The beauty, the struggle, the kindness, all the things that built your fifty years deserved a voice. Also, there was a desire to get the news out to the first tier of friends and family so that they could then carry some of the responsibility of expanding the circle of this heartache... so they could share in the delivery of this, saving us from carrying the pain alone. With the need to talk and share our experiences, it quickly became necessary not to relive it every time we talked to another person. Somewhere in there is the balance between wanting to talk and not wanting to talk, between the help from sharing it with friends and the avoidance of pain caused by delivering the news of your death... yet again.

YOUR FUTURE PLAN

From your own words, you discussed feeling like a burden to Mom and Dad (no matter what they would say to the contrary). You had requested, if you were to die before they did, that you did not want to have a funeral service. I imagine that decision was intended to save us the pressure of putting one together... and maybe to ease your own mind over the thought of having a viewing when your friends and family could actually see how your thoughts and condition had treated your body, and vise versa.

It was almost as if you had lived your life in an attempt to not really be there... from your refusal to sleep in your bedroom, to your rare appearance at meals with Mom and Dad, to your ever increasing tendency not to complete any work, to the obvious state of your diminished body. After your death, in your desire to quietly drift away with little notice, you had eliminated a place where we could all grieve together, where our friends could come together and feel that they could do something to ease or at least share our pain. Without that, we now have to relive the experience, our feelings, and our pain each time we discuss it. With each bouquet of flowers, the knife gets twisted a little more. With each sympathy card, the scab gets ripped open again and again, although, I'm not sure that the goal here should be to avoid pain. In much of the human experience, yes, but with your death and in the way you died... it might be best to fully feel all of the pain and sorrow, to submerse ourselves in the heartache.

As I was told once about the pain of a lost love, "The only way around it is through it." This, in some way, is why I am sitting here writing this.

Most of your life was devoted to your work… the work of creating beauty. Contributing your illustrations to brochure covers and advertisements eventually lost their attraction for you, but your drive to paint beauty never changed. After your career of focusing on commercial work, it was the bigger, the more permanent creative outlets that drew your attention. Creative outlets such as murals, portraits, a world trade center design, and in the very end, designing for stained glass windows became the purpose for your life. As I think of it, the evolution of your work was consistently towards projects that would last longer and longer. An illustration for a brochure cover ends up in a landfill or recycled within a year or two. A mural lasts as long as the business or the building. Portraits live with a family, but after a generation or two may find their way to a dusty attic. Your world trade center memorial design… maybe a year after 9/11. Well, this one hurts the most, maybe because your image, although probably one of the most beautiful (and possibly most expensive) structures that would have ever been built in this country, took a year of your time and could never have gotten through the bureaucracy, the red tape, and the "committee design" that the United States now faces in almost every task. Lastly, the stained glass design. This would have been a perfect fit. Traditional stained glass designed for churches is a respected and lasting art form. And your work, the preliminary ideas and sketches that you developed to enter the field were… well, at the level of the best stained glass work from any century. You were moving towards more and more permanency in your work. I only wish you could have realized that any steps back into a career can't be made up with one piece of work. You burnt yourself out with each project, striving for perfection. In the end, each piece was left unfinished and the next "solution to a failing career" was taken on. It hurt so much to watch this pattern. Not just because it was good work that would never see the light of day, but also because you were stressing yourself way beyond anything that could be considered healthy. You were a stubborn woman, and for good or bad, had always made your own choices. I think that statement is a little misleading. You were always extremely kind, caring, and attentive. You listened to anyone that you chose to give your time to, and when they spoke about themselves, you were always supportive, calm, and thoughtful. When the discussion was about you, you would also listen respectfully. You then pretty much ignored the words of others and did what you wanted, but always with the indication that you heard and thought about what was said and always with a very logical reason why your plan was the correct thing to do. And with each successive project, you made the choices to give yourself less sleep, less food, and less social contact... less life.

In the end, organ donation was not possible. Giving your body to science was another wish of yours, but the autopsy, the infection, and the hip operation made that impossible too. I wondered why there wasn't a medical center somewhere that wouldn't want your body at least to show students what happens with anorexia: "Look class. This is what happens to a body in cases of extreme anorexia. Aside from the effects on the bodily systems that broke down one by one, look at what a healthy body and a vital life can become. Never look the other way and never dismiss this disease as either unimportant or as something to simply ignore." Once again, there was a hope that someone might learn where you couldn't and a hope that all this pain might have some benefit to someone somewhere.

After being declined for organ donation and a donation to science, cremation was our last choice. Mom, Dad, Chanin, and I sat in a slightly tacky room at the funeral home. I don't know why, but the aesthetics of funeral homes always seem to be a cross between a casino, a brothel, and a church. We talked through issues like what newspapers to place the obituary in and what "burnable" coffin to place you in when they pick you up at the hospital and what urn to get. Flipping through the catalog, we looked through all the different, mostly overly flourished and awkwardly ornate urns. It was an attempt to give you the respect by choosing the "right" one. There was also still a desire to avoid this whole process. It seemed so casual, so ordinary, as if we were picking out a toaster oven or a vase from one of those "Everything for Your House" store catalogs. The selection of urns was a perfect match for the decor of the funeral home. After a little time, we finally settled in on the least gaudy one we could find. It was a simple wooden box with a leaf texture on the sides and an engraved brass plate on the top. I don't know if it was our emotions talking, some higher form of reality, or simply an attempt to believe that there was an urn that we could actually "like", but we found ourselves saying things like, "Kim always loved nature. She would like the leaves." A few days later, we would have to come back and identify your body so the funeral home could be sure they were actually cremating the right person. The process at times became morbidly surreal and oddly practical.

At home that night, I drafted a death notice. It was partially written out of pain and partially out of the anger about your death, and maybe an attempt to help someone else before it was too late, but I wanted to talk about the cause of death. Yes, I could have side stepped the issue, the pain and the social stigma about it, but I felt the need to tell the truth, and at the same time, respect you and your life.

I realized, for the first time, that there were death notices and there were obituaries; two separate and different statements. I normally don't spend much time in that part of the newspaper; actually I normally don't spend much time in a newspaper at all. Reading some of the notices, I was annoyed by their plain vanilla approach to describing a human being. There were no personalities, no indications of who these people really were, just: "Name, died blah, blah, blah, left behind, blah, blah, blah." If that was the general information that was needed, I wanted to just touch on who you were, and in the process, spare our parents from having to write their only daughter's obituary.

Kimmerle C. Milnazik

Painter / illustrator / friend

Kimmerle Cheryl Milnazik, 50, of Wayne Pennsylvania, passed away Friday morning at Paoli Hospital. She leaves behind her parents, Robert and Janet Milnazik, and a brother, William.

Kim spent her life in pursuit of creative perfection. As a graduate of Tyler School of Art in 1977, Kim developed a successful career in illustration in the Philadelphia community. She had an extremely detailed style and she was one of the few artists that had a deep appreciation and understanding of the works of the masters such as Rembrandt, Church and Ingres.

Kim was a very kind and quiet woman who always had a kind word for everyone. There was always an interest in the lives of friends and family and she always gave good advice without the slightest hint of any judgment. Kim was the kindest soul we have ever known.

As her career began to wane, she focused more and more attention on the perfection of her skill. In this time, a struggle with anorexia grew. Through family attention to this over many years, we eventually felt some optimism and possible hope of a path out of this illness. But complications after a broken hip led to her death.

Kim's life was simultaneously beautiful and sad. She tried tirelessly not to burden her friends and family, but through this, she unfortunately kept her struggles private. She had a very delicate footprint on this earth and leaves a huge hole in our hearts with her passing.

The trip back to the funeral home was our final chance to see you… our final chance to look at your face, to see the child and the sister that would no longer be part of our lives or our world. It was a large room, formal with its ornamentation and subtle pink and gold tones. It was intended for large gatherings of people who would be there to say goodbye to a loved one. Normally filled with soft conversations and the emotional support of the many that would be there to give their regrets and condolences, when we walked through the door, we saw the emptiness of the room. Off to one end were a draped table, a coffin, and your body. There are so many times when the simple images of this process create an irony that symbolically describes your life. The solitude and emptiness of this room was yet another. It didn't take long, but the tears started to flow as we looked at your lifeless body. With your grey, taut skin, you took on the appearance of our grandmothers at their funerals. The accelerated and self-abusive life you had chosen to live aged you way beyond your years. This was not a funeral, so they didn't put the effort into making you as "beautiful" as possible. They did use a few of their basic abilities to keep your mouth and eyes closed and it was a much less painful last image to have in my mind than the memory of what we watched at the hospital. But all I could feel was the immense, almost physical pain of this sadness.

A SNAPSHOT OR TWO

Nana was the name we gave to our grandmother, or more likely, she chose it and gave it to us to use. She used to take us out fishing on the lake. We were two of a very limited number of children at the old and wonderful club in the mountains of northern Pennsylvania. In its origin, as a hunting and fishing club in 1900, only men would go there to drink, hunt, fish, and play cards. As the years passed, it slowly opened to wives, children, and grandchildren. We were not the first, but we were part of an early wave of youth that came to the club. In many ways, this was where we grew up. Summer vacations and weekend trips held the wonders of hiking, fishing, swimming, learning to shoot; all the things that one associates with the outdoors experience. Family style meals were eaten in a large dining room with all the members. It was a time to talk about the day's events or just laugh with friends. In some ways, it was the large extended family that we never had. We explored, we had crushes on the children (or grandchildren) of other members, we grew friendships, we sailed, we learned to drink for the first time (or at least I did), we went swimming in waterfalls, and we gathered friends for late evening trips down the pitch black road for bad pizza and beer (in later years of course). It was a place that held many of life's new experiences for a young person.

As kids in the back seat of our silver 1964 Chevy Impala, we would try to hold our breath when driving through the one-mile tunnel on the way up to the club;

we'd have staring contests to see who would blink first. At the club, either we would stay in the lodge, a late 1800s hotel that overlooked the lake, or in the small but comfortable upstairs room of our boathouse. Those days were filled with the excitement that only young children could have about the new and unknown events that a vacation can bring. We would spend hours fishing with Mom and Dad, or Nana, and occasionally Pop Pop, although I think he liked more solitude than two young children could provide when seriously fishing. Out in the small boat, it was time to relax, talk, and watch the shoreline for deer or otters. At about seven years old, I realized, after a number of examples, that my fishing improved if I fell asleep while holding the fishing rod. I also remember sitting out in the middle of the lake on one warm summer night with you and Dad, with more stars above us than I had ever seen, or have ever seen since. We just sat out there under the stars and talked. The image in my memory is still as bright and sharp as ever.

It was an era when just sitting in the evenings playing cards was time well spent. In later years, you taught me to water ski. Being a couple of years older, you learned first, but when I was actually standing "on the water" for the first time, it was magical. Every day, you and I spent hours out in our white Owens speedboat. It was probably built in the '50s with a hint of a couple of stylish fins in the back and a forty horsepower Evinrude motor that was plenty for skiing until both the motor and I got a little older. My adolescent aging added size and therefore weight, while the motor's age decreased its power. But aside from skiing a little less, there were no cares, no concerns, just getting the most out of the days we had there.

Probably my first memory with you was being dressed up in some Easter attire of shorts and suspenders. The outfit I'm sure was a very cute parental decision but any photographs of it would still be embarrassing, even at middle age. There were Easter egg hunts and the joys of Easter baskets filled with chocolate rabbits and jellybeans and always that large chocolate egg that opened to reveal the treats inside. We would spend hours going through the baskets, comparing and trading one thing for another depending on our whims and favorites at the time. You always liked coconut; I never did.

At Christmas, we would wake up, or rather you'd wake up first and come into my room, not willing to wait for me to rise on my own time, and we'd both run downstairs to see what Santa had brought. It was a classic or almost cliché experience that happens in so many households across this country, and I wouldn't have had it any other way. I still remember the specific sound of my footed pajamas scuffing across the hard wood floors. Mom and Dad wanted to enjoy our reactions while we opened our gifts but because they didn't want to get up at whatever ungodly hour we did (possibly because they just had spent half the night putting together a bike or some other thing that we absolutely "needed"). As a result we learned that our Christmas stockings were open turf for us to explore before they got up, but nothing more. Any gifts under the tree were off limits until they joined us. I now look back and see an image of Mom thinking of what little low cost but interesting things she could throw in our stockings that would keep us busy and allow them another few minutes of sleep. When they did wake up, it was a tradition of classical Christmas music, orange juice with sherbet in it, and attempts to take turns opening gifts, or at least that is my image of how it went. There may have been more chaos than I've chosen to keep in my memory. Family and friends would come over in the afternoon. For so many years, our house was the gathering place at Christmas. Family, friends, and kids at Christmas—what could be better?

There were a couple of trips to Florida with Nana and Pop Pop and a number of what I look back on as "larger" vacations. One was on a sailing boat in the Caribbean for a week, when, I suspect, the price was well below anything one can find now. None of us knew much about sailing a boat that size, so Matt, the Sea Otter's owner, and Anne, his wife, were the captain and crew. You and I had the front bow bunks and we talked about what we saw during that day and what we were excited to see the next. I was twelve and you were fourteen. I think there was just a hint of an older sister losing interest in both the exploration that a young boy does and the thought of being around her "little brother". Lying in the sun listening to music became some of your main interests at the time. This was before any news of skin cancer, and the thought of premature aging from sun exposure was unthinkable at our ages. With every evening anchored in a different cove, I saw it then and look back on it even now as an incredible family trip.

We grew up as typical children of the '50s and '60s. I played army in the woods with friends, hunted for crayfish in the local creek, or built forts in the woods. Of course, like so many little girls of that era, you had a prized collection of horse models on your shelves, loved pink, would go to girl scouts and spent hours talking about boys with your friends. Through middle school and high school, we began to drift apart, as many siblings do. Both gender and age fueled this separation. It wasn't out of any disapproval of the other; it was just that the immediate interests of each of us steered us towards a different set of friends. In learning how to become adults and individuals, we simply were doing so in different directions.

In later youth, you had a drive that grew out of a simple interest and into a burning curiosity to find out what you could create in any number of different media. Paint, metals and fabric were all the raw materials of creativity. As one beautiful creation after another came out of your mind and hands, we began to see your talent and your love of creating beauty. It was a love of "something" that could be a marketable skill, and there were growing reasons to think that you had the ability to make this your career. A career that their child loved— what else could parents want?

When I chose to make art my calling and chose to attend Tyler School of Art, we reconnected over the goal of learning to improve our skills as artists and determine where in the wide range of creative options a career would reveal itself. There were times when we would each walk to the other end of the hall to ask opinions of each other on our work in progress. It was the start of a respectful adult relationship and the discovery of our own different creative styles. But at the time, there was just no way to know what challenges were ahead...

... for all of us.

WHAT TO DO

It was Mom's suggestion: a commemorative show of your work. It seemed to make sense. You had devoted your life to your work. I would frequently look at how you would strive for perfection, or rather how you would approach your work, and even with your self-built prison that kept you from the life you deserved, it was still what you held closest to your heart. Your early career produced some great illustration work, and we were all proud of you, but we also would have easily traded in that creative talent for a happy and healthy life for you. When someone's drive becomes a destructive compulsion, it's easy to think that the very compliments of early success become the choked back fears of fueling a self-destructive fire. Kim, I knew, as we put together your commemorative show, that you'd probably be up there fidgeting around saying, "No, not that piece," "Don't show that," and, "That one isn't ready." I thought for a moment of the urn with your ashes sitting in the living room. It's in front of the large window that overlooks the backyard where we played as kids, a room where the Christmas tree stood for so many holiday seasons. I could imagine the urn wobbling and bouncing around from your uneasiness at our travels through your work or maybe at the thought of showing what you all too easily discarded as an embarrassment to your ability. Well, Kim, I have one thing to say, if you wanted a say in this show you should have stayed here to be part of it.

We found a location on the way back from our first visit to the funeral home. It seemed perfect for you and your work. St. Aloysius Academy is a beautiful

49

building that started as the estate of George Childs, the owner of the Philadelphia Public Ledger, in the early 1900s. In the 1940s, St. Aloysius School for boys purchased the estate. In recent years, they have begun to rent out the main building for events. With its thick stone walls and carved wooden beams, it just fit your sense of history, your personality and your aesthetics. Even if the idea of a show tormented you, this location must have quieted what we assume would be your unease about showing your work. As we were walking through it, thinking about the logistics of work placement and traffic flow, Dad said, "This is the kind of place where Kim would have liked to live," and in an odd way, you now will.

After a couple of weeks of numbness, pain, and the inability to put any real answers to the question of "why", we started looking through your studio. Our initial goal was not to "clean out the basement". Mom was not ready for that degree of elimination, and I too, thought that process was one that needed time and respect, both for you and for our need to absorb the event of your death slowly. We needed to look for the work that would be in your commemorative show, work that would deliver your thinking, talent, and brilliance and maybe hint at the struggle that also served as the barriers to the life that you truly wanted and deserved.

Stepping down the basement stairs brought a new and awkward feeling. How many times in the past had this same action led to the sight of you sitting behind your drawing board? How many times had I been greeted with a pleasant, "Hi, Bill," from you? I have a belief that when people work with tools or in a space for a long time, they somehow impart their souls into the tools or location. I've felt this when wandering through our great uncles' cluttered old barn and woodshop as a child or when working with their old woodworking tools today. I've felt it when walking into old barns in Bucks County or when I've picked up an antique camera or looked at the antique sewing machine that our great aunt Lottie would use to sew corsets in her youth. I felt it here too, although, it was more than the familiar "soul" of a

50

place of work in the past. It was mixed and confused with the sadness of a life taken too soon.

You always had everything arranged, not like the typical compulsive person one thinks of who lines everything up or measures perfect distances between their pencils or other tools. You didn't have time for that. There were illustration boards and panels hanging from the ceiling on pulleys for easy access, adjustable so you could work comfortably. Research books and papers were with each incomplete project. Palates of oil paint were all pre-mixed, waiting for the appropriate need. Glass pieces were cut as an in-progress stained glass study. Storage spaces were filled with past creative interests. If anyone else had seen it, they would have assumed that there was an extremely productive person there with a wide variety of interests. To us, it only served to turn the knife in our already open wounds of many years of failed attempts, discussions and offers of help. It was the visual manifestation of all your struggles ripped open and laid out in front of us.

We saw the figure of the lion head that you sculpted because the two years of drawing sketches and gathering references wasn't good enough. We saw the beautiful painting for the Philadelphia Opera Company disassembled and in an early stage of recreation even after it had been finished once, bought for the promotional poster and printed. There were revisions and tissue sketches for everything and endless photocopies of reference material that might be needed for all the work. There was a detailed line art border sketch that must have taken two hundred hours for just a preliminary tissue sketch with the intended use on a portrait that was left incomplete. In retrospect, it makes a lot of sense that you didn't finish; the degree of work that you felt was necessary for any project almost guaranteed incompletion. Your image of what could be was not going to be limited by the reality of time or budget.

Each pile of sketches brought back the painful memory of that particular phase in your evolution through your years of self-destruction… the attempts to coach

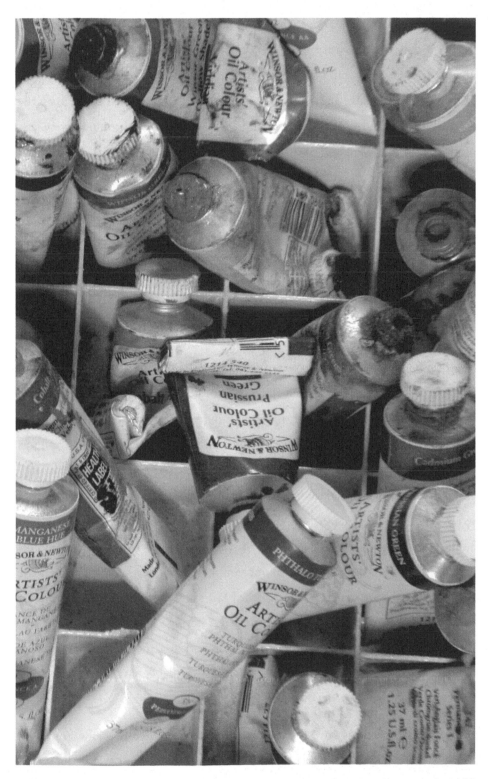

you out of your challenging logic… the pain of hearing time and time again that you only wanted to try this one last thing or that you knew what mistakes you had made and would work to correct them… only to give us one more example of compulsive and self-destructive behavior. We looked through all the corners, the boxes, the rolls of paper, and we were shown a more complete visual path of who you were and how you thought. Up until this point, I had never thought a piece of art could hurt so much.

When I was in college, for a couple of summers, I had a job with a moving company. I enjoy thinking back on that job for a number of reasons. Aside from the obvious physical exercise and the memory of a youthful physical ability that has, well, I'll just say "lessened" in my life, I was able to learn about people from the things that they had and the way they placed them. It was a study of psychology. Items of pride were placed in a central, easily seen location, like family photographs, expensive sculptures or religious references, and the things that were hidden usually defined their view of a "shameful aspect of their life" like nude photographs or awards for something like best employee at a fast food restaurant. Of course, we the movers, whose responsibility it was to pack things up, were not governed by the simple hiding of things. We had to pack everything, and a discovery of a little personal treasure only added a spark to the workday that would later be talked about over a beer or two. Either way, I learned that much could be gleaned by simply observing the "things" of a personal existence. This was no different. I learned more about you after your death than I had in the forty-eight years we shared on this earth. I felt sadness and pain, not simply for the loss of my sister, but now for the pain and suffering that you chose to live with in an unnecessary silence. In order to get the work together for a show, we had to relive the pain, the years of your unconscious suicidal behavior. It was a sort of time capsule of your work, your thinking… and of your illness.

Like the workplace of anyone who has an intense desire to make anything, there was what looked to be a balance of intense organization and the casual placement of the tools and materials that didn't need immediate retrieval. Some things, like your brushes, paints, pencils, and the glass cutting tools, were all seen in a basic organized and logical placement. Yet it was the actual work that seemed to have a degree of disrespect. Yes, they were rolled up. They were placed in boxes or put away, waiting for some future time of understanding and completion. The tissues were taped over each other in perfect order of creative evolution. On each layer was a sketch that showed a deliberate and calculated improvement over the last. The perfection of an arm curve here, the adjustment of many versions of a flower stem there, but there was a scattered, almost disrespectful placement about all of them.

I think what struck me most was an explosion of ideas; too many to stop and finish anything, more than any single day, or mind, or life could hold. Your time was the crucifix on which your very life was nailed. It was the limit that you refused to accept.

The endless sketches with endless layers of tracings taped to the surface showed the attempt, and honestly, the reality of an improved evolution in the work. As a creative family, as artists in our own right, we saw the thoughts, and for the most part, could agree with your choices. But it was also painful to witness the prison that you had built for yourself with this demand of nothing less than perfection, a perfection that could (and now can) never be achieved. Perfection in art is an admirable but mostly unattainable goal simply because aesthetics can't be measured and the definition of "success" in art has no limit. You worked as if it was not only possible, but with just more effort, it was within your reach. The real dilemma for us now was to come to an acceptance of whether the impossibility of achieving perfection was from your illness… or from your death. One holds the hope of a possible answer; the other is resigned to an unchangeable fate.

PERMANENCY

It seems to be a common thought with many deaths: "How can we give a more permanent and enduring meaning to a life that has ended?" Some people make huge and ornate gravestones or mausoleums, some create an endowment for some cause or another, and some have bridges or sports stadiums named after them. We were no different, although it had to be scaled down to the finances of our family.

In your final years, you would take occasional trips out of the house for supplies or references for a project. At one point, you decided that you wanted (or needed) to learn how to draw the human figure better. It was a pleasure seeing your enjoyment from the multiple classes you took at the Pennsylvania Academy of Fine Art. Something as little as seeing you get out of the house and take the train into town gave us joy... and once again, a little hope. To hear you talk of what you had learned made us happy with the obvious pleasures of seeing a loved one enjoying an aspect of her life. It also held the secondary and rarely seen message of you taking an action to increase the size of your world after letting (or making) it shrink to an unhealthy size. I have to say that I find it hard to believe that there was much of a lack in your traditional training. Between collage and doing some medical illustration soon after graduation, your attention to the human form, with the muscle and bone structures, was never something you would take lightly. Whether it was an extension of your illness—deciding once again that you weren't skilled enough—or just out of sheer pleasure, you were out in the world that we so wanted you to experience.

As a result of what we saw as one of your last successes at bringing a little pleasure into your life, we decided to put together whatever size scholarship we could to the Academy in the name of Kim Milnazik. After a few phone calls, a representative from the school came out to the house to talk over the options. We had thought generally about this before and had mentioned in your commemorative show invitation that any gifts could be made to this scholarship.

We had enough to help a single artist for a year or to possibly help a few artists over a number of years. Eventually, after a mix of personal, emotional, and financial discussions, we decided on giving a small grant to two of the best students over the period of a few years or more, depending on how long the scholarship money would last.

I have this image of the students receiving the scholarship and having possibly a slight knowledge of who Kim Milnazik was and why this scholarship exists, but they can never understand the depth of the story that put that financial support in their hands. Maybe it's not important that they do; maybe it is best that they can be lifted of some of the financial burden and given more freedom to explore their creative potential. It does feel good to help artists learn and improve, especially with the economic and governmental challenges that artists face at this point in time. But it also feels correct to honor an existence... and a sister that deserved a better life.

"GOOGLED"

A logical reaction to a death in current times is to see what affect this person has had in his or her life. What was done? What was he or she involved in? How is he or she seen on the Internet? After a quick Google search of your name, we came across a number of listings, some talking about various commissions from your earlier days as an illustrator, but most as companies selling reproductions of your work, making money from your ability when you couldn't. A short explanation of artistic rights is probably needed here. When an illustrator is commissioned to create a piece of art for a client, there is usually a negotiation. The client can purchase the rights to use the art for a single project like a brochure cover or advertisement, they can purchase unlimited use of the art for a given period of time, they can purchase the original painting to frame and place in their lobby (or anywhere else), or they can purchase the copyright to the art, allowing them to sell rights to others for uses ranging from specific promotional projects to reproductions of it as fine art. There are all kinds of variations on these options, and like with a lot of things in life, it forces us to become at least casually knowledgeable about legal issues. This describes the basics of the process, and each purchase method has a different price attached to it. It originally started when clients would pay almost nothing for an image, saying it was only going to be used on a matchbook cover or some other small project, and they would then base an entire advertising campaign on it, gaining large amounts in increased sales but having paid almost nothing to the creator of the art. Therefore, laws were changed to protect the rights of the artists. Think of it as someone who writes a new piece of software that makes life easier for many people. It could be copied and distributed easily for free, but the creator of it does have the right to control the distribution and to get reimbursement by those who use it; otherwise, what is the impetus to create anything, aside from the warm fuzzy glow one gets from exploring his or her own abilities. But one can't eat a glow.

The Google listings showed many companies selling your work. To be fair, I know that some of them had made a legal contract with you to sell your work for that purpose and some companies might have purchased the copyright for a given piece of art, allowing them to sell the rights to anyone they wanted for any use, but the selling of a copyright is not common. It usually costs considerably more since it can prevent future income for the artist with the reselling of the image for other purposes in the future. Unlike credit reports or security alarms, there is no automatic way for an artist to know when his or her possessions (the rights to his or her work) are being stolen. It is up to the artist to monitor this, and it's literally impossible to look at every avenue of unauthorized sales. The legal implications and penalties when someone is caught are the main deterrent, but I have to wonder how many of these Google listings selling your art are making a profit illegally. They profit on the shoulders of talented and struggling artists or, in this case, on the shoulders of one that might have lived and found a way out of an illness if the financial struggle had been less of a factor.

FLASHBACK

It was a trip to D.C., my gift to you for your 34th birthday. We drove down for the weekend and toured the galleries. It was an attempt to get you out to see a little piece of the world. We had time to talk, time to relax, time to get away from both our normal lives and to a place with the best collection of museums in the country. In that time, Mom, Dad and I were just beginning to think about the possibility of anorexia or bulimia with you, but we really weren't sure. This was before we noticed any real struggles with your work. Not that they weren't there, we just were not exposed to them yet. It was inevitable; at meals I would watch what you ate, looking for any piece of evidence of a problem. I remember being quietly surprised when you actually ate quite a bit, and I wondered about the obvious, when you got up right after eating to "go to the bathroom". It was the early stages of our observing, wondering, while trying to respect your decisions and privacy. There was a discomfort with even the thought that I should be watching you or doubting your words that "nothing is wrong".

The first project that made me think "Something is wrong here," was a mural for an auto body shop. In looking back, I realize that there are natural chapters or simple designations of time created by the different projects you were working on. Unlike the traditional auto body shop, this one was clean and upscale, and they wanted a large mural for their lobby. It was to be a beautiful arrangement of a collection of twenty or so of the world's classic cars, some appearing as ghostly shapes, some partially shown, and some complete in their beauty. The border was a very involved Art Deco style. There were endless sketches with assemblies from many tissue paper sections taped together. This is not uncommon in the creative process, yet when nothing was completed, we began to see that you were getting stuck in the process of perfection, in the planning of a single piece of work rather than in the evolution of a career.

The second project in a series of work that now seems to take on the image of painful dysfunction was a large painting for a client and fellow Tyler Art School alumni. It was a painting of a tiger for her business. The business had a related name and a big dynamic painting would have been a great asset for their lobby. It hurts me now to even think about it. There were two years of research and sketches, only to end in your frustration that you could not get any reference with the correct lighting and angle. I remember saying, while knowing all too well that you could have used this to take another two years for exploration, "Why don't you sculpt one yourself? Just a rough version." This was an important and carefully injected statement for you in an attempt to prevent you from obsessing on perfection there, too. You did sculpt a nice little, and for your sensitivities, rough version, but this project fell by the wayside, only to have a regular reminder of the process with the four by five foot sketches hung in your studio. I don't think that it was a loss of interest on your part—maybe an acknowledgement that this one had to be put down for other attempts that might produce self-sufficiency. There was an ever-present requirement of us, a balance between support for your work and practical business help. I wonder at times if we were actually helping at all. Was our understanding of the aesthetic drive and our recognition of artwork and its value a liability in directing you out of your destructive cycle? Were we blinded by our own creative sensitivities and the value that *we* placed on the artistic process?

A commissioned series of portraits was the next project. It almost seemed logical. Portrait work could almost fit in perfectly with your independent nature, and it usually didn't require a tight deadline. It was for a family with three children.

You were to paint each child separately. And in this, too, I saw brilliance coupled with a compulsion not to release your goal of perfection. I think in the end, the sketches went to the family at no cost and the paintings sit partially finished and completely reworked in Mom and Dad's basement.

Somewhere in the series of projects, there was a portrait of Princess Diana. It was done soon after her death and you felt it could be timely to send out a promotional piece with the goal of revitalizing your illustration career. This one was completed. I remember it taking a while, but it was completed, and it was a good piece of art. It must have been hard for you to let that piece of work end. Printed copies went out in the mail for self-promotional purposes. Soon, you were on to the next task, forgetting that human contact (sales) was a critical part to selling custom work of almost any kind.

I think after that was another painting done only for your portfolio. Artists do this. It's a way of showing what they can do even if they haven't been given that type of work for a commission piece recently. What hurt was that you had plenty of good work to show. To me, as your brother and as one who would buy this type of work, it seemed that the problem was never your ability; it was your viewpoint of your work: the unattainable goal of perfection. From my perspective, I wonder if there was a lack of self-esteem from not reaching that perfection that made you need to work more and more in areas that had no evaluation from the outside world, financially or otherwise. Art is an easy obsession that way. One can work indefinitely at anything and tell himself or herself that it's all in the name of honing one's skills for a future delivery to the world. This is an argument that we had listened to frequently, and maybe accepted too many times. But it was a beautiful painting, a simple and elegant arrangement of lilies.

The next piece that comes to mind was probably your last commissioned piece, and one that was completed... sort of. The Opera Company of Philadelphia

wanted a painting for the opera *Tosca*. It was to be used for a promotional poster and pamphlet for the opera. The project came with a deadline and you managed through endless, sleepless nights and a renegotiation of the deadline to deliver what was a stunningly beautiful painting of a tormented woman from the opera. It was beautiful, yet the woman possessed an expression of anxiety, right at the moment before uncontrollable crying. Or maybe, she was showing her determination to not let those emotions out… ever. I used a close up of the woman's face on the invitation to your commemorative show and on the cover of this book. In a sad and beautifully ironic way, it captured the emotion of a suffering woman… of you. Like so many points, and with this one too, there was a quiet hope on our part that this successful illustration might start to show you that you could fit into the world, to let you know that you had a tremendous talent and that it was your own mind that was limiting your success, whatever you wanted that success to be. Maybe we all are held back by our own minds to some degree. We have these personal views of who we are and what we can do, and we try to live up to, or maybe down to them. So with tickets given to you by the opera company, you and Dad enjoyed the evening, as both the audience, and in a way, as part of the performance. I loved seeing you experience real life and aspects of fun. Each time—and I can think of only a handful—I hoped that you might see that you deserved a full and happy life. But each time you returned to your self-imposed prison, with a smile and the thought that, if you were to work hard enough, you might be able to justify a little of life's fun. After the performance, from across the room, the president of the opera company called your name to introduce you to his associates. I can only imagine how wonderful it must have been to receive that acknowledgement from a world so much bigger than the one you were shrinking into. There was acknowledgement in front of people who valued your level of creative brilliance, and I have to think, from a business angle, the purchasers of fine paintings too. The conductor wanted to buy the original painting for his personal collection. "Oh, I need to finish it first; it isn't ready for selling as a fine art painting." And it too, sits in the basement, cut apart, disassembled and treated as so much photocopy paper whose only use was to get your work to some unknown artistic level.

9/11. America will never be able to hear those numbers and think of just some average day in some average September. It was that event that moved us all to think, to feel, to question the value of what we were doing. From a large American political level to the small personal evaluation level, everything came into question. You were no different, with the exception that you approached this with your set of skills and worked for the next year to draw up plans for a new World Trade Center Memorial without a concern for your day-to-day life. The open contest for ideas gave you another open-ended task. It was honorable. It was valid. And it was another "project" that had only the hint of an "end" based on the deadline for submissions, but even that deadline was extended and you chose to work beyond that time anyway. "It's important," you said. "Just let me finish this and…" There were always negotiations, always "how abouts" and "what ifs". It is that very enthusiasm that was so hard to shut down, or to redirect. How do you strip someone of her true love? It was at this point in time when I began to think that it really was up to our family. No therapist or doctor was able to stand up to your kind and unconsciously brilliant form of manipulation. Doctors were either afraid to deal with this type of disorder and/or maybe just bound by HIPPA to act out of privacy but not necessarily on the patients best interest. We were individually swayed by your amazing set of negotiation skills, so a regular family meeting might have been the only tactic that could have directed you back to a real productive life. "Productive", I was beginning to think at this point was just to be self-sufficient. Your memorial sketch was, however, a beautiful design, and I even saw your attempt to rough things in as a time saver. Was this our influence or your weakening body and mind?

After all these projects, the idea of a new direction took hold. Somehow, you decided that designing stained glass could be a direction that might suit both your temperament and your ability. At a family meeting, we discussed it. The walk along this tightrope was one of the most difficult I can remember with you. On the one side was the fear of yet another endless avenue of research that you would all too often follow. On the other side was the fear of killing your heart and soul by not encouraging you to try something new. As the years and discussions had passed, I had begun to focus more on the best and only way I could approach you, with strong and honest thoughts and opinions, worrying less about hurting you than simply delivering what I was seeing. It's funny sometimes how long it takes us to do what should be an every day occurrence, honesty, direct honesty, and supportive honesty. Openly fearful and based on past experiences, it was all on the table. It was an approach that, in the past, I had tried to follow, but now it seemed to be growing in importance as more and more years were passing with no positive movement. I believe that people who have the fire burning in them for almost anything are halfway to success. You had that fire. It was very sad to see that energy choked by the years of shame and disbelief in your own wonderful ability. Was that shame from our years of attempting to directing you away from your own self-destruction? Was it an understanding of your failures and possibly a fear that these failures were not simply isolated issues but rather symptoms of a much greater problem? I guess you, too, had a balance to walk—one of excitement for the future and acknowledgement of the past.

The learning began. There was a stained glass conference about two hours away that you wanted to attend. When we heard that you wanted to drive yourself there and stay over night, there was a magical, uplifting feeling and an acknowledgement that this feeling was over something so simple and small yet enormous for you. For you to choose to be away from the house, away from your studio, and in the company of a new community of people made us so happy. This was extremely atypical, and it showed the desire to stretch out past the tiny little life that you insisted upon for yourself. We had tried so often to get you out into the world. "I don't have time," or, "I need to work to make up for my mistakes," or, "I don't have the money," were your usual answers. I think Mom and Dad paid for the car and I paid for the room, or vice versa. It doesn't really matter.

I remember being surprised that you had even renewed your driver's license. You had chosen not to drive for so long. You would get rides when possible or walk miles rather than drive again. Years earlier, it was the accident, caused by your excessive working and lack of sleep. It resulted in you falling asleep at the wheel, the loss of your car, and more importantly, one more step away from life. One of the first things that I noticed when you came back from the conference was a lightness about you that we had not seen in so many years. You had an excitement, a new direction, and a new skill set to learn. You said that all stained glass designers needed to have a decent understanding of the production aspects of the process. This is typical for design related professions. But I would be lying if I were to say that I wasn't afraid that this would also become an endless series of basement projects, all "teaching" you what you needed to learn but never ending in a self-sufficient life. We sat down as a family and discussed it from all angles and with all feelings, fears, and concerns on the table. Our support was there, but it could not be open-ended one more time. We had bent, shifted, and moved time lines so often in the past. This time we gave you a deadline to work within. If that time passed with no employment, you would have to do what everyone else had to do: put your attention toward self-sufficiency in any way possible. If this meant getting a job at a bookstore or any other basic employment where you would have regular hours and an interaction with the outside world, so be it. You agreed.

As time passed, you did what we expected and feared and fell back on the only thing you knew. You devoted twenty hours of every day to your "work". But as you gained knowledge in the stained glass process, you began to make contacts with businesses that build and refurbish stained glass for churches and other large installations. Their comments to you were often that there are people that produce and construct stained glass well but there are very few people that have the understanding and creative design sense of the past. You held these qualities, and your love of the past brilliant "masters" gave you the aesthetic knowledge that these companies needed. This was beginning to finally look like a fit for you and your work, a path leading away from the struggle and pain. I remember after the first of a few interviews with one company, you mentioned that the owner initially said that he only had ten to fifteen minutes to meet. You walked out of an exciting first meeting after an hour and a half. When one is so compromised in her self-worth, a small event like this can be a beautiful and inspiring gift. After the second interview, you were given a trial project to work on. I don't think we ever said anything to you, but in the back of our minds, we were hoping that this company wasn't stringing you along in order to get free ideas and designs. Anyone else could have handled a disappointment like this but for you, you needed and deserved a "win". As the time got closer to the deadline for this project, again, you took the only approach you knew. You worked longer and harder. There is no doubt in my mind that you had completed this many weeks before but you had to be sure it was perfect. You had to be sure that this would get you to a productive path… that you would be hired. The alternative was too painful to think about, so you worked. I think it's human nature, when we experience a series of failures or "bad luck", that the importance of the next success grows beyond what it would normally be. This anxiety about success sometimes causes the very result we are trying to avoid. We found out later, after your death, in a discussion with the owner of the stained glass company, that they were in fact, very serious about hiring you and loved the talent that you could have brought to their company.

I'm not sure exactly when this picture was taken or where, but this is how I remember Kim; loving, gentle & sweet. I so looked up to Kim because she was so beautiful in so many ways. She had a regal grace and a soft voice and I hoped I would grow up to be just like her. My fondest memory is when she was 19 - that became my magic number because I thought at 19, she had everything. She was talented & so lovely with gorgeous long brown hair, high cheekbones and light blue eyes. I'm sure I drove her crazy with exuberant admiration & adoration but she was always gracious & patient. The world is a sadder place without her but there :3 celebration in heaven.... JoAnne

FLASH FORWARD

In the basement, underneath the stairs, was a locked chest. I think it was the one you took to camp when you were about twelve years old. It was a short trip. The camp looked good in the brochure, but the reality was more along the lines of an abandoned military base. It was about twelve hours after dropping you and your friend Denny off that we came back to "rescue" you both. It was a call from Denny that talked about cockroaches, rats, and the first day's chores of cleaning the outhouse; it just didn't quite create the camp experience for a young girl that you or anyone else expected.

There was a curiosity about seeing the lock on the chest. Like any locked container, there was an implied hint of importance to whatever was inside. There was an initial thought of looking for and maybe finding the key, but the reality of the situation was that we had more important things to do than search for a key to a $25 chest. The pain of traveling through your possessions weighed heavily against any of the more practical thoughts.

After a little work with a screwdriver and a hammer, the lock broke loose. We thought that since it was the only locked place in your studio it must have contained something of importance, something that you held dear to your heart. As I lifted the lid, my first words were...

"This

Dad had spent his career as an illustrator and graphic designer. I can hardly remember for how many years, but he produced calendars that he used as self-promotional pieces. They usually had themes and showed the beauty of his thinking, illustration and design ability. He was one of the great designers/illustrators in Philadelphia from the '50s through the '80s. There, on top of the chest, was a collection of his calendars, along with a single annual report that I had designed in 1989. It was an annual report that I always loved and that showed an understanding of the client's message and a connection to a visual artistic style of the past. In this little example, Kim, you viewed our work above the endless examples of your beautiful creations. It was a grasp at your thinking at best, but it hurt to think that you placed your work below those who would have done anything to show you your real worth. Let me stop here and say that the truth is that I would have welcomed with open arms a sister who had done absolutely nothing creative but was happy. You could have had any job—working at a convenience store, as an office administrator, or just about anything. It all would have been desirable over your demand of yourself... and your eventual death.

After we had lifted samples of our work, at the very bottom of the chest, we found pieces of your past success. There at the bottom were the metal printing plates from a college project. It was a book you had done, illustrating the story "The Emperor's Nightingale". You were young, energetic, and driven. You would take on a project in a way that few would have attempted. Not that one can describe your work by a simple subject matter. It was more what you chose to do with it. The complexity of illustration and production for a college project was

is going to hurt."

amazing. At the end, I think the class required twenty-five books to be printed and hard bound, most of which are scattered amongst friends and a couple are in the hands of book collectors. So there, in the bottom of the chest, were the printing plates that you needed to make and use to print that book. Ironically, a few finished copies were found in a plastic wrapped bundle in a corrugated box in an opposite corner of the basement. As we looked through the plates, we found about twenty-two plates for the complete book. I wondered if there would ever be a need for these plates again.

We collected work—some prints of past work, some sketches of future ideas, some paintings of your thoughts and dreams, all pieces that would become the show that you never felt worthy of. Taking the work up to your old bedroom, we laid it out, grouping it into work that would be framed and matted, and photographic prints of older work that we thought should be mounted on foam board. I guess I had gotten used to seeing your room in a perfect condition, not because you had left it that way, but because you chose not to use it, to be closer to your work… no matter what we would suggest, ask, or speak about. Your bedroom was actually more of a guest room. "Kim's room" was merely the name it acquired from the years of our youth. And now, after your death, we were bringing elements of your life back up into it.

CALIFORNIA NO. 1

Since we were two years apart, we shared time throughout much of our school experiences. In high school, you were the artistic star, and I was, until my senior year, merely dabbling in the art room. Like many young boys, I was more interested in how to say hello to the cute girl of my interest. In my case it was Meredith, a crush lasting through most of middle and high school, although in my awkward youth I was too shy to do anything about it. Of course, there was the obligatory time spent in sports (pole vaulting on the track team) and "cruising" up and down Lancaster Pike (when gas was 37¢ a gallon) learning how to grow up and maybe how to avoid it at the same time.

It was a typical suburban school experience in the '70s. Get up after a few calls up the stairs from Mom, each a little stronger in emphasis than the previous call, have breakfast, walk out to the bus stop, which was just at the end of a neighbor's driveway, climb onto the obligatory yellow school bus, and pretty soon we were walking through the doors of Conestoga High. With about seven hundred students in each graduating class, it was larger than most schools in the area at the time. A school of that size could offer more specialized education in different areas. There were simply enough kids to justify a better and more diverse school experience. We had no adversity, no real troubles, other than the typical youthful challenge of navigating adolescence.

In looking back, that was a time when you seemed to shift from a young girl who had friends, went out, dated, was a color guard for the school sports teams, and who loved art, to someone who had this drive burning, a drive  to be good or maybe great at your creative work. We were fortunate enough to have a well-rounded creative experience there, too. We experimented with ceramics, painting, sculpture, metalworking, and obviously drawing. Jeff, one of the art teachers at the time, was instrumental in "lighting our creative fires". To this day, some thirty-plus years later, I think back on that time and am grateful that we had teachers that opened our eyes to what the creative process could be. It wasn't about painting or drawing. It wasn't about clay or metal. It was about seeing and opening the mind to think in new ways, to learn that not knowing the answer and the process of finding it was where the true fun of the creative process lay. I will always be grateful for Jeff's influence and still tell him that when I see him from time to time, although I suspect he may be tired of hearing it at this point. I had a very difficult time calling and telling him of your death. From his forty-year experience of teaching, there are many memories, many student creations and many faces, occasionally one or two that just explode with their newly acquired creative direction. You are one of the students that he thinks back on as one of his best.

My friend Mia also knew you from high school. Mia and I met in our junior year and shared the fun of exploring our creativity in the art classes we had together. After another crush on her ended in our junior year ended with a very clear message of "Nothing more than friends, pal!" we became just that. Since that time, she has always been there for fun, for help, for life. Over the years, Mia has become more spiritual than I, and a lot of her belief has focused on the Native American spiritualism. This is a small and seemingly odd detail to throw in at this point. I know, but trust me, there is a reason for discussing this now.

When someone close dies, there is this extremely strong urge to understand, to know, to connect. There is the obvious sadness around that person's loss, but there is also a denial or maybe a need to accept his or her absences slowly. We can't seem to accept it all at once, so we talk to the person, we pray, even if prayer is not a common or familiar activity, and we reach out to find any way to feel less pain. There is a saying: "There are no atheists in foxholes." This may hold true in time of loss, too.

In more recent years, Mia has been combining her talent as an illustrator and her spirituality in a process of doing shamanic journeys for people and then painting a symbolic portrait of that journey for them. One of the things I love about Mia is her ability to understand that different people are at different levels of understanding with spirituality, and without avoiding her beliefs; she is able to talk to anyone at his or her level. It is a rare ability. After your death, I was a little reluctant, but I asked her to do a journey for me. I guess it was like asking a friend that is a house painter to help you paint a room. People spend so much time in their paid professions that it just seems rude to ask the same thing of them as a favor. Nevertheless, I was so lost in my pain and wanted to know something... anything about how, why, or possibly even whether you are okay now... a never ending question ever since man rose from an animal of basic survival and began to ask, "What else is out there?"

A shamanic journey is like a meditative state in which one is open to dialogue, imagery, or any other information all based around a few questions, a topic, or person. It didn't require me to be there with her in the process. It was done in Mia's own time and space. But that is my extremely limited understanding of it. After living with my own pain, any information at all was needed. I was driving up to Doylestown to see Chanin when Mia called to tell me what she had received from the journey. It was about forty-five minutes of tears in the car listening to her results of the journey. A few days later, an email came through with a written account of what she saw, heard, felt… or maybe I should just say "found out". There was a comfort to hearing these words. If it was the feeling of still another connection to you after your death or a little piece of understanding that this, too, was just how it should be, or maybe both, it gave me a momentary calmness that I hadn't felt since your death.

Question:

Is there anything that you would like to share with Bill that could be of help to him with the pain of your loss?

Answer:

She shows up right away. I see her on the coast of California out on a little spit of land that overlooks the water from high up on the cliffs.

She invites me to sit with her. She looks so beautiful that it's beyond words. The first image she shows me is an image of her braid in your mom's hands. Her braid (a piece of it) sits in a row of other braids from those ancestors who have already passed. It has something to do with being cared for in a way that was the same with these other women. It may also be that she wants you to know that she is in the comfort of these others, who have been waiting for her. She shows me her personal journal that has a letter inside an envelope. She said it's okay if you read it. Now I see her dressed in lavender and midnight blue. She is stunningly beautiful. She shows me that she has now fully embraced her power and essence as a woman. She just glows with confidence. I ask her if there is something that you might not understand that would be helpful for you to know right now. She shows me a huge rock that she is turning over. Underneath are all of the trapped soul parts. She waves them to come to freedom. They fly off and are free. When I ask what these figures represent, she quickly responds and says, "They're me!" She lets me know that these are soul parts that are all freed, all the parts that were once a part of her but trapped.

I see her collecting seeds, one at a time. Then she shows me a metaphor about plants. She wanted you to know that she was like the houseplant that does very well outside in the summer for one season but cannot thrive in this environment all year long. She wants you to know that her time was meant to be just the way it was. She came here to be who she was and then her time was over and it was time to leave. She repeats, "This is the way it was always meant to be. My time here was never meant to be any different."

I go to meet one of your guides to ask about Kim and an elder shows up. A Chief Elder (Native-American-looking) shows up with a mask painted with white paint. I ask him about his mask, and he tells me that it's a way for him to honor his ancestors (those who have gone before). He says that this gives meaning and is a way to honor their lives. So, I ask if this is something he is suggesting to you to do, and he confirms with a yes. (This is why he shows up this way.) I ask him how you can do this, and he says that these things will present themselves on their own, a little bit at a time. He says that it happens in a varied way and to stay flexible about how it comes to you. He says that, at times, it will be like separating thin papers with tweezers and to be patient with yourself. It's going to be delicate work.

Now I see Kim sitting side-by-side with the Chief Elder. She shows me that she has been wearing a mask since she was about six years old. I ask your question again, and she says, emphatically, "If he's still smoking, tell him to stop."

She wants you to know that "it" was much bigger than her. She says that she was "engulfed". She shows me herself in a swirling body of water. Then I see that the family is on the banks of this river and she is in the middle of the river (in the swirl). She says, "If any of you had tried to save me, you would have drowned." She is so happy that you have all chosen to live. She is grateful that you did not risk your own lives. She wants you to know that she gave everyone the only thing that she could give: hope. She said that she knew all along that it was bigger than her. She told me that her leg hurt her all the time (left leg?) before she broke her hip. She really did understand that she was near the end of her life but wanted to give comfort in the only way that she knew she could: to give hope. I ask her one last time if there is anything else that you need to know that will be of help. She shows me herself holding hands with lots of children. She is radiant and happy. She shows herself like a Mother Teresa image and then like herself again. I am getting ready to say goodbye and thanking her when she reaches out and hands me a rose to give to you. She wants you to place it over your heart to remind you to keep your heart open. Then she blows a kiss on the rose.

CALIFORNIA NO. 2

Prior to your death, I had scheduled a trip out to California to visit a very good friend of mine, Steve. He is the brother I never had and always seems to be a good sounding board, and although this trip would not be our usual fun; it seemed more necessary than ever. Self-employment doesn't leave a lot of time to travel, but I could barely handle any more pain, and I needed a break from the sadness or at least a change of location, some good conversation, and some support.

I love flying. I refer to times like that as being my own captive audience. There is nothing to do but think, write, listen to music, and read, all the things that I seem to miss in my day-to-day life. This flight was my own personal time to write, to try to add logic to the insanity of losing a sister that in many ways, I barely knew. It wasn't because I didn't want to know you but because you had shut yourself off from me, from your friends, from Mom and Dad, from everyone who might have possibly seen through your dysfunction to the caring and beautiful woman underneath and tried to help. But to be honest, I, too, get caught in my own work and life. So for me to blame our tentative relationship all on you just might be a little one-sided.

A beer at 9:30 A.M. is not a common practice for me, not nonexistent, but not at all common. In this case, I was way beyond adjusting my behavior to any list of rules and regulations. In the Philadelphia Airport, I sat at the bar, opened my laptop, and continued to write. It seemed, and still does seem to be, the only process that would calm the pain. In some ways, when I write, I feel like I'm holding onto a connection that inevitably becomes thinner and thinner with each passing day. I have discussed this with others and said that I have no idea what, if anything, this writing will become. I know that, as the pain, the confusion, the sadness, the grasping at ideas passes, I just want to document the process so I don't forget it… so I don't lose the connection to you.

About two hours and one beer later, I was on the plane. "Pull the safety buckle, blah, blah, your seat cushion can be used as a floatation device, blah, blah." A floatation device flying from Philadelphia to the first stop of Chicago. Hmmm. I paged through the magazine looking at all the cool gadgets that I will never buy. Finally, we were at an altitude where "electronic devices can now be used". I was back at peace with my thoughts and my writings. I have this belief that writing slows the thought process down. It allows us to focus on the trees and not the forrest and productively work through ideas and if one is really lucky, get to solutions. Fingers simply do not bounce from topic to topic as quickly as an unencumbered mind. Thoughts can be explored in a more logical and sequential order and possibly from a different and beneficial perspective. That was where I was for the next two hours. There was something very freeing about looking out the window, level with the passing clouds, and writing about you. Our traditional images of angels up in the clouds made me look out the window and with a slight smile, wondering… were you out there?

The next leg of the trip was fairly uneventful for one reason: the battery of my laptop had run out. I was forced back into the world with everyone else—in-flight movies, bags of peanuts—but still the calmness of being able to just sit and think was a welcome change.

I had been at Steve's place for about two hours, talking through the pain and emotions, when I got a call from Chanin. Her dog was dying. Hershie had become a good friend to me, and he was her best friend. I had comically accepted the fact that I was second in Chanin's life. Now, with his passing, I was unable to be there for her. I realized two things that evening: (1) It's hard to know what to do with friends that are in emotional pain. There is confusion as to whether to let them cry and embrace the emotional state or whether to try to shift their emotions from their pain through laughter or diversion. I understand both tactics and the thoughts behind them, but I have learned, in that moment of devastation, to let them cry, let them feel, and let them be with their sadness completely. It can be a little disrespectful to try to change someone's thoughts because one is uncomfortable with the tears or pain of another, or maybe it's just a matter of not wanting them to hurt. A kind thought for sure, but as a supportive friend the best thing to do is just be with them. (2) The second thing I realized was that sadness is not simply an additive process with one source of sadness adding to another. Now I was not only dealing with my sadness of your loss but also the loss of Hershie and the fact that I was so far away from Chanin when she needed me the most. Each layer of sadness works as a lens on the other, multiplying the emotions. I began to see how people could lose their grip on reality in similar situations. Is this what happened to you? Was it the same process that happened over many years? Was it an inability to recover from each impact in life that led to an ever-loosening grasp on your own reality?

So once again I cried, not knowing if it was for Hershie, Chanin, or you. It was probably some combination of all three. And I thought *Hershie is a dog, one that has had a long and wonderfully spoiled life. My sister had a life of hidden torment and struggle, and it ended all too soon. How can I possibly compare the two?* The truth was that I couldn't. They were all valid reasons to be sad, and any attempt to portion out emotions based on the importance of each death was just my own desire to honor each with just the "right amount" of feelings. They can't be measured. We can't say, "This event justifies thirty-five percent of my sadness, so I'll have sixty-five percent left for you." It all blends into a stew of emotion, and the complexity of that stew is what makes us struggle, and it's what adds to our humanity.

The weekend was filled with the right mixture of conversations and, the occasional diversion. We hiked, talked, ate, and drank. We even laughed a little from time to time. It was probably my first hint that I might be able to feel normal again. My original plan was to fly back Monday, but a late breaking business meeting kept me there until Tuesday night. It was a little odd; the day after I made my flight reservations, a client called and wanted me to attend a meeting in California that Tuesday. Weirder yet was that the meeting was twenty minutes from Steve's home.

When Steve also had a sudden business meeting come up on Monday and had to fly out of town, he said, "Take the car and just explore." After dropping him off at the airport, I first went back to his apartment and just sat... thinking about your death, your life, and what we possibly could have done differently. This has been, and will continue to be a recurring question. After about an hour, I decided to go to the beach. The beach has always been a place of thought and contemplation for me. In the past, I had a tradition of always taking my birthday off. I'd drive a couple of hours and go "talk to the ocean". I don't know if it's the solitude, the visual expanse, the regular meditative sound of waves, or something else, but I always feel better around the ocean.

After getting lost on a few of the roads below Los Angeles, I found myself driving south next to the ocean towards Laguna Beach. The road was surrounded with a lot of low scrub brush, an occasional cactus and some very "well healed" properties. I noticed a sign for a state park ahead and pulled the car in. The guard was noticeably helpful and pleasant. I always find it interesting to meet nice people when traveling. There seems to be a lack of them back home, or maybe it's just around urban centers where the volume of people in close proximity place a tint of frustration over life which leaves little for most casual meetings. After pulling into the gravel parking lot, I walked out along a long wooden path through the dry plants and the occasional lizard running across the boards. It was a curving path designed specifically for the aesthetics of the walk. At the end was a deck, fenced in so that sightseers wouldn't fall over the seventy-foot cliff down to the beach. Standing for a while, I watched a few tiny ships in the distance and a scattering of a few people here and there down the beach. In this environment, I might have been looking for the hand of God to come down and open my eyes to the real purpose of your death. Needless to say, the clouds didn't part, no booming voice from above and no message of comfort was delivered, but it was pleasant to just sit in the warm sun, feel the pacific breeze, listen to the waves and

"talk to the ocean."

I must have spent about twenty minutes in my aquatic conversation. I stood to say goodbye to the waves and return to the car and the day-to-day existence of Southern California traffic. As I got up and turned to walk back, I noticed a small path that went around in front of the deck. Curious by nature, I followed it. I found myself walking along the edge of the cliff. There were no railings, no fences, just a carved out sandy dirt path also about sixty feet above the beach.

Down below was the typical collection of Californian beach materials: rocks, tidal pools, and just enough sand at low tide to create a beautiful walk for the people I watched below me. As I walked around another bend in the path, I saw something written in the sand below. It was hard to make out, but the first thing I recognized froze my feet in the dirt. It was the name "KIMM". Oh God! Okay, Supreme Being. Okay, whoever is in charge of those great coincidences or those direct and intentional messages from beyond… thank you! I didn't see any other people nearby, just your name written in the sand… and a second "M" that I could choose either to be from the spelling of your name (Kimmerle) that was taken from the last name of a family friend of Mom and Dad, or for our last name, Milnazik. I stood and looked at it for a while, trying to take in a meaning, a message, or just the enormity of this little scribble in the sand. After staring and thinking for a while, I walked a little further, around another bend or two, and found a single bench with a beautiful view of the Pacific. The sound of the waves, the warmth of the sun were comforting enough, but I somehow felt a little peace that went beyond the normal ocean "buzz". In these times, we may very well search for and find the meaning that we need, but seeing your name in the sand seemed to send a thought to me that you were okay and that you were reaching out to me in a wonderful way… and at a wonderful time. Mia's reference to "finding you" on a cliff in California brought further meaning (and maybe questions) to this experience. As I walked back, passing your name in the sand, I looked again and read what was under "KIMM". It was clear as could be, and I wondered why I had not been able to read it before. It was one of those times when an agnostic would begin to believe in something greater. Just under the word "KIMM" were the words…

"I miss you."

THIRTY DAYS

It's been a little over one month since your death. In that time, there's been a swirl of different emotions, most of which I can do little with, other than observe and endure them, although I am beginning to wonder if there isn't some value in each and every one.

I've thought about this analogy and have decided that it is fairly accurate: When you died, it was as though a cannon had blown a hole through my chest, leaving nothing but emptiness. I initially tried to feel anything, but sadness was my only option. I reached for any other emotion… and failed. Being a practical and, at times, overly logical man, I found it strange and difficult to feel this way. I was no longer in control of my life, thoughts, or emotions. You and I were unfortunately not that close. This was partially due to your illness and the way that you'd always hold me and the few remaining connections in your life at a distance. To look at it honestly, I too made choices. I was either absorbed in my own life or maybe had just given up trying at times, but all of that kept us at a distance. I do know that your separation wasn't built out of anger, resentment, or anxiety. It was built, either consciously or subconsciously, to protect your approach to your career, and it was built out of a stubbornness that served to reject anyone's offer of help. I know that in your own mind, it was what you felt you needed to do. You had the one solution to your career problem: work harder. Although I will never know, I also wonder if your distance was also a method to keep us from opening the door to your most private possession: your illness. Anorexia lives. Like a virus, it has a way of protecting itself while consuming its host. It delivered such low amounts of nutrition to your brain that you actually believed you were healthy and productively working to solve your career pitfalls, and you believed that we were wrong in our twenty-plus years of talking, advice, concern, and requests for doctors and therapy. Anorexia kept you sane enough to avoid complete failure and being placed in a mental institution or being committed to some place that might just force you to get well and eliminate this demon. It also kept you sick enough to allow it to continue its consumption of your body… and mind. A parasite unlike any other.

I suppose it's the way things are supposed to be. As time passes, I hurt less. The sharp pain is turning to a dull empty sadness and the inability to have almost any emotion. Fortunately, I am able to look at this time as the cost of passage through this emotional quicksand. It's not a time to fight it. It's not a time to struggle, to avoid the pain. It's a time to accept every emotion, every thought, and every feeling. Faith has always been elusive to me. I have always wanted proof… although "proof" kind of eliminates the very concept of faith—belief in something that has no proof. Yet I now freely believe that I am not in control of how my heart and mind choose to heal from this. I am in the hands of some other force, and it knows best what path I must take to heal from the pain. My only responsibility is to let go and feel what I feel and think what I think and to believe that this is the best path through the pain. I suppose this could be considered some primitive, single-celled, preschool form of faith.

There was a day or maybe a moment when I first noticed that I hurt less. The next emotion I noticed was guilt. "Is this lack of pain minimizing your importance?" "Am I mourning enough?" "How much sadness and pain is one supposed to feel?" "Am I allowed to smile or laugh yet?" These are questions that I last remember thinking after September 11, 2001. And now, one month after your death, they revisit my mind. I find an occasional smile on my face, laughing for a few seconds with a client or friend or actually forgetting about your death for a moment or two. It might simply be the human nature of self-protection. A body and heart just can't feel that badly for that long. I don't know if depression is a result of habitual thinking of sadness for a long time, carving its deeper and deeper grooves into a single thought process, or maybe a consistent release of some chemical into the body as a result of emotional struggle. But I do know that for me, aside from writing, letting my thoughts take their own path and talking to people that care is the only healing method that will work. Yet, for you, letting your thoughts take their own path was your downfall.

On April 3, 2006, Mom called. "How do you feel today?" It took me a second to realize that it was the one-month anniversary of your death. I don't normally focus on anniversaries of events. Having never had children, I can't know what it's like to lose a child. But I realized that my process and Mom's process through this would be very different. I can't condemn dates to permanently relate to the day you died. I can't view the world in relationship to what was or what could have been your life. Yet I completely understand how my mother may want or need to think this way. It's a slower release of you. It's a method of relating to you even after your death that lets her stay close to you and then ever so slowly saying goodbye and releasing you in the smallest of units, and over an ever-adjustable amount of time. It's a way to let the hole in our hearts, and the emptiness we feel, slowly heal, the way some injuries are left open so that they can heal from the inside, gradually filling in the void. There is an odd comfort from knowing that pain is still a connection to you, but the healing itself is a slow loss of that connection.

PISSED

I was so furious. It was an anger out of frustration, out of fear, out of the feeling that you were holding our family hostage and that you were continually wasting our time with the illusion that you were actually listening to our thoughts and suggestions. You chose not to support yourself. You chose not to eat. You chose not to get help. And you chose not to listen to us. You chose to spend insane amounts of hours on tasks with no chance of any financial return when you were not able to support yourself. You chose not to sleep. You chose to shut off any connection with friends. You chose to tell yourself that you deserved nothing. You chose to die!

It would probably have been another movie cliché if it hadn't involved so much human suffering. Someone falls into a difficult situation. Friends and family rush in to help and support, but with no evidence of an attempt from the person to help herself, the support dwindles. After some time of no change, frustration rises. Anger and then separation. I tried so hard not to just write you off. After twenty-five years, I suppose I can say that I did my best at continually trying to help. But there were many times when I needed time to step away, to regroup, and to build up both my strength and my optimism. There were many times when I just

You Chose to Die!

had to not be around you. I apologized to Mom about this, and I apologize to you now, but I simply could not be pulled into your dysfunction for any more than periodic visits. I found that, from time to time, when I just couldn't watch your choices or listen to your dismissal of our help, I had to be away from them for a while. This could have been weeks or more, and I felt guilt about it each and every time, guilt for not being there for you and guilt for not being there for Mom and Dad. You each needed very different support.

So many times, I questioned if we had gone way past the support and help needed to direct you back towards the vital and productive life that all of us wanted for you. Your thoughts were not missing from that equation either. You talked of wanting a life of independence and even let yourself dream of wanting a few of the simple pleasures in life. You rarely let yourself want anything, but these little seeds of wishes were signs of hope. After some time and after endless offers of support and help, I began to wonder if we had become enablers of your dysfunction. I wondered if our actions, in an attempt to help were in some way actually allowing you to stay exactly where you were. This is one of the many challenges when dealing with someone with distorted thinking, and I was angry with you (and all of us) for being in that position.

I worked hard, if one can actually work at such things, to move away from that anger so I could deliver help and think logically about how to effect a change to a very entrenched thought process. I found that I needed to let that anger out with other people. Not towards them, but with them. I found that, over time, I was less likely to "cover up" for you. I was less likely to change the subject to protect your reputation. I was becoming honest about what was happening in our family. That honesty came out with others in openly talking more about how I was feeling, and it came out more towards you, too. I did my damnedest to keep my frustration away from you, but I also tried to openly talk about what I was thinking and feeling. You were a stubborn woman who would all too often figuratively "back hand" those that loved you and were trying to help you, but we always thought that it was not a deliberate disregard for our suggestions. In your head, you so tightly held this path of a solution and were simply blind to any other possibilities. Or maybe, what effect we actually did have, moved you in inches when we needed to see miles. But you were also an extremely fragile, caring, and loving woman, and pushing hard seemed so unfair.

I began to view your soft-spoken nature as another form of manipulation, and I was angry with that too. I also began to develop an anger toward myself. How many times did I feel like the fool for trusting in your words? How many times did I hear a logical and calmly delivered solution or a plea for more time only to have it result in the same immobility and another new and unfinished project?

When you were alive, I saw this anger as justified. It was the energy that kept me (and maybe you) focused on possible solutions. We are of largely German and English heritage, nationalities that seem to connote a reserved and introspective method for problem solving. So a fiery Mediterranean temper is not part of our make up. Anger takes a very different path for us, or at least for me. I feel it; I look at it from different sides; I pick it apart and try to separate the valuable and truthful pieces from the reactionary and nonproductive sides of it. Overly analytical? Maybe. But for right or wrong, I have always felt that it's a better approach than jumping down someone's throat.

This process may have contributed to why we took so long to slowly increase the focus or intensity in managing your condition. I know other families that, after a year, might have said, "Get out and figure it out yourself!" or, "We don't owe you anything anymore. Go sleep on the sidewalk." Would this kind of "tough love" have been a better approach? Would this have forced a change early on, possibly resulting in you learning to find your own way out of this disorder? We will never know.

It was so easy to be angry at you,

at us, at the seemingly hopeless situation when you were alive. As long as you were with us, I felt there was always some possibility of an answer, however minute. I could not give up and accept that you were simply just mentally ill, rendering you incapable of living your own productive life. You were creative, brilliant, caring, pleasant, all the qualities that would give someone a wonderful and productive life... except one. And as long as I believed that there was hope, I was angry at the reality of you not stepping towards that possibility.

Another reason for my continued focus on your well being, and one that created a certain amount of shame, was that, as time passed and as Mom and Dad got older, I began to see that without an independent and self-sufficient lifestyle for you, there would be a time when I would carry the financial, physical and/or emotional responsibility for your life. This was something that Mom and Dad tried to prevent, and they began to research state help and where you could go if your approach to life were to remain unchanged. But I had to look practically at all of this, and I saw a time when either you would have to move in with me or I would be managing the finances and visiting you in some home where you could go to live out life. I'd put on a fake smile and pretend that I was happy to see you when the reality would be that the visual reminder of your collapsed life would rip at the ever-thickening calluses on my heart. Either way, I wanted to do everything I could to prevent this, and I had to remind myself that, if any help was partially motivated by altruistic feelings of support or by self-protective selfish thinking, it was still help. But with your loss, those very real, self-centered thoughts feel... just wrong, as if, without them, you might have lived. Although, I know now that would not have made a difference.

As the months have passed since your death, I have slowly let go of the anger toward so many different parts of this. It holds no purpose now other than to cast blame on someone or something for the pain caused by your loss. It doesn't serve as a source of energy to keep me focused on trying to help you anymore. This blame and this anger have no value, no use, and I now wonder... did it ever? In the final years of your life, did my anger prevent me from looking past your illness and seeing and knowing a sister that had so many good and wonderful qualities? Yes, you held yourself back from us as well, but in retrospect, what purpose did that anger serve? In retrospect, it's so easy to look at past events and adjust or change an opinion or thought. With your death, how can we not?

ANOREXIA WITH A TWIST

There have been many attempts to understand your illness. It's what one falls back on when any results or success seems too impossible to grasp: the thought that, if we can learn what you are going through, what you are experiencing… what you "have", we can find a way to help.

There were so many therapists, or at least as many as you would let us suggest, and every one had a different conclusion for what was preventing you from having the life you deserved. Schizoid personality disorder, anorexia and obsessive-compulsive disorder—the list grew ever longer with the seemingly arbitrary names for what we were experiencing with the confident, self-destructive, and amazingly calm and brilliant daughter and sister.

There is an inclination through all of this to come out with some clear and concise description of the disease and say that we have learned of a wonderful new way to cure anorexia. I wish that I could say this, but I can't. I can talk about my experience, I can talk about what I've seen and witnessed, and that is all. What I now believe, after years of being pointed at one diagnosis or another, each time thinking, *NOW, we have a real and named disorder to deal with,* is that you had a combination of anorexia and to a lesser degree, obsessive-compulsive disorder. Those two disorders brought a specific mix of distorted thinking and physical damage to your life. The two seemed to reinforce each other. An obsessive-compulsive disorder may have helped you to repeat the same unproductive behavior and with the absolute belief each time that it was the solution. Anorexia is, or at least was, rare in women your age (when you died), and when a decreased amount of nutrition is given to a body for that many years, there is not only a physical degradation but a mental one as well.

Many people will look at a problem with anorexia and say, "Feed her." A simple idea, and it might have an effect on the short-term mental distortion, but from everything I have heard, food is not the problem. It is a by-product of distorted thinking but not the cause. Increasing food intake (assuming that is even possible) is not fixing the underlying problem. I have criticized the medical industry here. This is partially from the frustration of hearing many different opinions, partially from the destructive privacy of the HIPPA regulations, and partially from the plain and simple fact that you are no longer with us. But I will say that, from this point in time, with whatever knowledge I have gleaned from years and endless attempts at finding a solution,

it is
serious!

It can result in death. It can ruin the lives of those who carry this challenge and can radically affect the lives of those around them. I believe that there are different levels of this, some very serious, some less so. In our case, if I were to wish we had done anything different—and this is difficult to discuss, because it brings with it the "fault" of not taking one action or another—I think we could have taken a more serious approach earlier. A possible tact would have been to send you to a center that dealt with this for a week, a month, whatever. There

are a number of places that specialize in eating disorders. I would have liked to see you in a longer-term environment in which you could have seen and talked with others that were carrying your life's challenge. HOWEVER, as an adult, you had the right to say, "No," and you did.

Another piece of information that has been suggested to us, albeit after your death, is that there could be some connection between scarlet fever as a child and compulsive behavior later in life, and you did have scarlet fever in your early years. Was this a ticking bomb waiting to go off at some point in your life or a force that was simply stronger than any support or help?

Okay, I have to write a very strong caveat here. Any medical opinions written throughout this book are just that: opinions. I am a brother not a doctor. To talk about your life, to discuss the difficulties that we have experienced and to talk about your death, some degree of emotional and medical information has to be discussed. But no specific approach or medical expertise is assumed or even suggested here. Everyone has his or her own path with things like this. These writings are only delivering my experience and my thoughts and opinions.

HAPPY HOLIDAYS

Time gets ticked off in so many different measurements. Days, hours, minutes, and seconds are all called upon to build a structure around our lives. What we can accomplish in a specific time period indicates a degree of success or failure. Years add wrinkles; the sunset connotes either slowing down to a dinner with the family or maybe time to gather friends at some restaurant or bar. After a death, holidays immediately become another way to measure time—the first Christmas after a death, the first birthday, the first Thanksgiving, or any other regular family experience that has acquired a meaning by the repetition over many years. Personally, I have a love/hate relationship with holidays and did even before your death. We—and I mean the big American cultural "we" here—have made most holidays into another reason to buy things we don't need... to feel an obligatory responsibility to smile more, to expand our circle of well wishing way beyond our ability to deliver real and honest emotions. I look at other people's experiences with holidays and wonder if it's real joy or a case of "The Emperor's New Clothes", in which nobody feels the right to say, "No." The first series of holidays without a family member does little for any feeling of joy. It mainly serves to remind us of the loss. It's a somber time and probably one of great value when we quietly listen to our emotions and replay our memories.

This was the case here. This also made it much harder to put on the public face that seems to be required when our country goes into Christmas chaos. It has

been a goal of mine to shrink Christmas down, to make it smaller and more emotionally close, to make it mine. Kim, the first Christmas without you left me with little desire to celebrate. I chose not to. I kept my head down and waited for it to be over. There was an attempt to be there for Mom and Dad. Now that I am an only child, I find that I feel an obligation to be there for them. And maybe, in some small way, I can soften their pain, as they can soften mine.

ONE YEAR

I haven't written for some time now. There have been holiday dinners with a missing family member, birthdays when there was no need for gifts, trips into Mom and Dad's basement, where there was no smile, no short talks, no catching up on each of our lives.

I think for me, the choice to avoid writing was out of a need to regain some control of my life and to think about things that are just part of day-to-day existence. Work has always been there for me. For good or bad, I can always focus on work and see an effect of that labor. Maybe it's that German work ethic from our heritage. My relationship with Chanin has suffered this past year. I can't pretend that this is solely due to my difficulty with your death. I know there are issues that she and I each bring to the relationship that cause problems, but I can't help but wonder if your death or my reaction to it has not partially contributed to an emotional "shut down" on my part. I have learned that, in times of stress (either for emotional, financial, or physical reasons), I tend to pull in, to focus on a smaller arena where I can create some degree of success. Life does go on in many ways after tragic events, both good and bad. The ripples from events in life can travel through years, decades, and relationships, and I think, in some ways, through multiple generations. Things are experienced; things are learned; things are taught and passed on to others.

March 3rd, the one-year anniversary of your death, was on a Saturday this year. I wasn't thinking that much about it. Any day is simply one more day than yesterday and one less day than tomorrow. How can a point in time signify more importance or a greater emotion than any other time? Emotion is emotion, any minute, any hour, any day. Yet, when I awoke that Saturday morning, I felt you in the air, I felt your loss, and I felt my sadness. The day was spent in the same way I always spend my thinking time: working around the house, making "my space" a little nicer, a little more interesting. It's a creative drive combined with the nesting instinct I guess. It also gives me time to think, to feel, to cry a little, to be alone with myself. I didn't expect to have this flood of thoughts, this wave of pain. The practical side of me saw no reason for it. I can feel sad about your death any time I want. A day doesn't change anything. But it did. And I have learned that it's best to let the emotions go where they need to… and when they need to.

I thought about what I was doing exactly a year ago—the phone call, the drive, watching the life leave your body, seeing the various monitor readouts slowly flatten, watching Mom and Dad as their only daughter was succeeding in the trickle of a suicide that was neither intentional nor conscious. Kim, I am still not right. I thought about my life and how your death has affected me. I assumed, or maybe falsely hoped, that by this time I could return to my life, and in many ways, I have, yet the anniversary, this tic mark on a time line, has brought me flashing back to the raw emotions of one earthly revolution ago. (Is that a little too cliché of a phrase? Probably, but allow me that for now.) As I sit here, candles lit, with the slight scent of wax, I look around my living room. Uncle Charlie's 1915 Excelsior motorcycle in the corner, an antique piece of stained glass that I framed and gave to you fifteen years ago in the window, an Edison phonograph from our grandmother off in the far corner, rocks sitting on the hearth, collected from a college trip to the Dominican Republic with my girlfriend Anne, a painting that Chanin and I did together on the wall, and many other memories collected around me. I sit with the souls of events and people past. The comfort is both palpable and new to me. I rarely stop and think, or maybe more importantly, stop and feel. It occurs to me that, if these writings ever see the public's eye in the form of a book, two messages might be distilled out of this: (1) The sadness and despair that comes from anorexia or any self-induced loss is huge and hurtful to so many more people than just the one directly suffering from the illness, and (2), the path through emotional pain is very personal and different for everyone. Most importantly, it's valid and necessary to feel that emotional pain, and experience it fully. This is a story, a message, a feeling, and an experience that I hope can be of value to someone, sometime, somewhere.

I HAD A DREAM LAST NIGHT

I was living at my old house, a small house, a simple brick twin built in the early 1900s. When I walked out the front door, you were standing in the street. You were thin but not nearly to the degree that you had been for the past decade. You seemed healthy, confident, and had a calm beauty of the Kim that I once knew—no pretense, no fear, just the friendly attitude of someone who knew who she was, what she had and what she wanted. You smiled and said, "Come here. I have to show you something." We walked a block or so, and you got in your car. I got in mine to follow you. You were driving fast (atypical of your past years in so many ways). When I tried to keep up with you around a turn through an intersection, I took it wide into the other lane. There were cars stopped at the traffic light, requiring me to stop and back up before continuing to follow you. When I came back into the lane, no more than a few seconds later, your car was gone. You had disappeared. You were either too far ahead or you had turned off someplace.

When I went back to the house, the adjoining property was being put up for sale. It had a lot of glass windows in the front and had the entire first floor converted into one large dining room. The real estate agent asked me to put a tablecloth on an oak dining room table that could be seen through my front window, an attempt to dress up the place a little for any potential buyers. Then everyone came into my house to take a look at it. It was a mess with half-finished projects everywhere. I initially was embarrassed but soon accepted that it was just how my life was going at the time.

And I remember dreaming about telling other people about my dream.

Kim, thanks for visiting me.

111

"PRACTICALITY"

OK, A death is a death. Most people, if they're lucky, have lived long enough and have connected with others enough to experience the loss of a loved one at some time in their lives. Everyone will die. It is something that no one can escape. To quote my ex-brother-in-law: "Life is a sexually transmitted terminal disease."

So, why obsess about death? Why spend all this time in these pages, either reading about it or, in my case, writing about it?

I think the reasons vary depending on who has died, how they have died, and one's relationship with that person. So once again, I can't speak for the masses here. I can't make words that resonate with all people who have had a loss. But I can talk of my experience with this specific death, with the sister that I loved, that I wanted to help, that I wished I knew better.

For me, your death was difficult, tragic, sad, and painful for many reasons. For starters, you were my only sibling. No matter how close we were or weren't, there are no others. No others to lean on. No others to share joy and pain with. No others that can know what it's like to lose you as their sister. I carry that alone. I have spent time talking to friends about my thoughts and experience with your death, but after some time, I feel that it can only come out in sound bites, short references to the acknowledgement of your death. A good friend of mine lost her brother to a suicide. It was more deliberate than yours—an overdose and a body found a number of days later. We now have a bond that neither of us ever wanted. But there is a comfort knowing that if I say anything, a short hint or a long description of my thoughts and feelings, she understands... as I do with her. It is a club, a club that no one wants to join, but every member is reassured that there are others who have shared the same initiation. At the same time, I would never wish this club membership on anyone.

I never want to become callous of any death, yet there are many millions of deaths that I will never know and thousands that will only be passing news blurbs, like a shooting in my home city of Philadelphia or the casualties of some meaningless war. But there is something about a self-taken life. Am I placing more importance on this because it's your life? Maybe, but whether it's an immediate decision to end one's life or suicidal choices that take place over decades, when a life ends at a person's own hands, it leaves much more than a death. I almost typed "simple death" here but "simple" is hardly the case. For the people left behind... and even more for the family that loses one of their own there are the questions, "Could I have made a difference?" "If I had been more of an influence in their life, would this have still happened?" I have heard these questions from the casual acquaintances that crossed your path and they ring loudly to those of us who were in your life for... well... life. I have had numerous discussions with people and read numerous e-mails that have raised questions like these, whether they knew you for life, for decades, for years, for months, or even in the short passing moments of a small few-hour event like my yearly summer party. You usually, but not always, chose to avoid it because you were "behind in your work", but connected so well with others if you gave yourself a few hours to enjoy a few new friends. The practical side of me thinks that love takes years to grow, but you touched so many, even though you tried so hard not to be there, to avoid contact with anyone in return for the solitude to perfect your skill.

There are those who look at death as simply the end of a biological existence—an interesting, and wonderfully simple thought that I have entertained from time to time. There are those who see life as a place where one scores brownie points for some future position in some religious place of reward after death. And there are those that see life as a temporary stage between the previous life and the next. I personally like to think of this life as a practice area that enables us to advance to the next level in the next life. It's a wonderful thought that we cannot only work and advance within this life but do the same across multiple lives and move up within our understanding of "the BIG picture". The truth is that I might, if I'm lucky, learn what really happens when I die, and I might not. I like to think that, when I die, I'll have the chance to talk with all those that have been important in my life and have passed on before me. Hell, maybe I'll talk with those that I am just curious to meet. A face-to-face conversation with Da Vinci or Einstein would be fascinating. Even with an adopted religion of one flavor or another, I can't really know anything about what happens after death, and without that, I may be even further from the truth.

So, getting back to death, your death specifically. Why does it hurt? Because you were in my life. Because you made a difference in my life. Because I cared. Because of all of that and the acknowledgement that you revealed about your life so close to the day you died hurt me too. And yes, I can look at it as a life that was ready to be taken. I can rationalize all of the different logical or spiritual reasons, and I can look to some unknown power as being both responsible and kind when it took your life. In the end, when there is nothing left but my own internal thoughts and feelings, when I've traveled through all the religious philosophies, the truth is simply that it hurts. All the logic, religion, and personal support only chips away at the thick layers of pain. No philosophy or religious belief can make any real sense of it or replace the work needed to travel trough the sadness. It's a death—unlike many others but a death and a loss nonetheless.

the truth is simply that it hurts.

In the process of writing this, I have gone from a need to explore my thoughts, feelings, and pain, then into thoughts of a possible beneficial use for these words in the future. The work required to reread, to edit, to complete areas that I discover are missing or simply a poor delivery of my intent does two things. It forces me to relive the experience through each and every edit. It also makes me wonder, is this focus on your life and death healthy? Am I approaching this in the same way that you approached your work, never letting it go? Maybe, but as an important and very sad story, and the first venture into a more complete written delivery, I think I'll give myself a little slack and simply follow the path before me. It appears to be a path of healing, understanding, acceptance and trust.

GENESIS

Given a little distance and the ability to look back, to search, to analyze, well…
to take a somewhat educated guess at how this all became real, I am left with a
few thoughts. First, life simply dealt you a shitty hand and you were left with
no way to understand the problem, let alone find the way out. Second, this
was many years of experience that built this life—a life in which, in the end,
your very approach to it became the ever-tightening noose for you. And third,
some genetic line-up flipped the first of many dominos, and the outcome was
never open to change. From this distance, it can be a little easy to be callous at
times, but that emotional defense has been well earned. For the record, Kim, the
dominos are still falling, even now, over a year after your death. They are just
seen and heard by others now.

Kim, you grew up with a creative drive that treated you well. As your brother, I
always saw you as the one who had the appreciation of others. As a young child,
you always managed to devote your time to something of value. I would often
joke with friends that "My older sister didn't do a very good job of breaking
in my parents. That job was left to me." At the time, it was a funny way of
saying that you didn't push them much. You were always the good child and
usually did not only what was expected, but more so. You were the overachiever,
the creative producer that delivered serious works of art. You had patience and
would spend a lot of time learning how to paint in a formal and beautiful style.

I, on the other hand, was the second child or, maybe more importantly, the youngest (and only) son and had a little more "play" in me. It took me longer to realize the career that I loved. Although from college on, I have worked very hard in my industry, and at times, have wondered if I too, don't carry some degree of the very philosophy, the approach to work that killed you.

In your youth, before there was any hint of a problem, you gained the appreciation of so many when you created a beautiful painting or a wonderfully ornate copper and brass incense burner in a metals class. I suppose it could have been anything. It could have been sports, academics or science... except that, with art, it's a process through which there is inherently no end to the possible improvement. There is no goal which, when reached, you can stop. The practice and improvement of an aesthetic career requires one to always question decisions and to always search for a better solution. And with Mom and Dad being artists, it was natural that they could and would appreciate and support your efforts in that area. I know they did with me.

It seems to be a positive aspect of parenting (of course, this is spoken from one who has no children, so armchair parenting is the best I can do); encouragement helps a child grow with self-confidence. It helps a child feel that he or she can then go on and try to accomplish other goals. Did you come into life with a damaged self-worth? One that, with encouragement in one area, resulted in your entire self-worth being wrapped around your art? But who doesn't grow up gravitating towards the abilities that he or she is better at? Everyone leans towards and gets more positive feedback for things they do well. In that sense, your life was no different.

In our early years, that adolescent formative time when kids absorb everything in front of them, we grew up in what I look back at as a sort of sixties modern society. Mom and Dad were not strict. I have this feeling that we were raised with a lot of open space to make our own choices. Not to the extreme of other people whom I know had absentee parents who, out of guilt, let their kids do just about anything. It was more of a deliberate choice to oversee us, to make sure that we were learning and experiencing life but also, as the years passed, with a growing amount of distance, letting us explore our own lives and desires. With all the variables in parents and children's personalities, and with all the societal changes and whatever the latest advice is on how to raise children, I often think about how difficult it must be to be a parent. How are parents to choose what is best for their child? How are they to determine which child's actions could be the sign of something serious that needs their attention and which actions should be left alone for the child to learn and grow from? And how much of a parent's own likes and dislikes should be passed on, let alone viewing oneself introspectively and helping a child to not adopt some of the less productive traits that we all have. Yet so many people seem to simply have kids out of some primal or obligatory reaction without thinking at all. Kim, in our youth, you were the one that always did the things that got appreciation. Creating beauty does that. Art is some mysterious thing that gets people to look, to see, to think. It has always drawn attention. And since the mysterious quality of art is one that is hard to define and often not questioned by a large part of society, it was the perfect place for your disorder to hide. Your obsessive drive, as its dysfunction grew, was easily hidden behind the dutiful artist at work. In many cases, this drive did actually make you a better artist. You built quite a reputation in your early years after college as an illustrator. Even then, I felt that you were living your dream and making great art as a living. To start right out of college as a freelance illustrator took a lot of courage. It required a tremendous amount of sales, taking your portfolio around in person to anyone that would buy these services, delivering confidence, talent and a personality that appeared easy to work with. This was before the Internet, when the design and illustration fields were much more than a commodity shown on a website. It was about people, ideas, and talent. On the other hand, when I graduated, I chose to get a regular job at a design firm. I think I learned a lot from that

IN MY MIND'S EYE, WE'RE ALL STILL 19 YEARS OLD — bright and shining, filled with hope and promise, some more talented than others...none more talented than Kim. She wasn't like anyone I'd ever met before...nor since, for that matter — poised, poetically beautiful, not of this time.

I was thinking the other day about our Tyler Prom. Kim thought we should have one, and so we did. She thought it should be beautiful, and so it was. She thought she would make and wear a dress based on MY FAIR LADY, and so she did. She wanted to create a magical evening and memory for all of us, and she succeeded brilliantly. That's what she did. That's who she was. Kim created magic out of thin air, beauty out of blank space.

I was very sad when we lost touch so many years ago and tried to maintain contact without infringing on Kim's privacy. Occassionally I would get a response or a message of some sort, but eventually that stopped as well. I've always believed that there is no greater gift nor heavier burden than an artistic talent. There is ceratinly no one more talented than Kim. I'm sorry that the burden was so great and couldn't be shared.

When I think of Kim, the first thing that comes to me is her voice. Funny, isn't it? I always talk about her remarkable visual talents and yet my first thoughts are always of her voice — very soft, so delicate, and wonderfully musical. That is my constant memory and one that I hold dear.

— Bill S.

employer, but it was sprinkled between years of drudgery and being held back by any number of boss's or client's fears that doing something interesting and noticeable could be seen as radical or inappropriate. That is after all, the job of graphic designers, to get their clients noticed and to have their correct message delivered… to separate them in the eyes of their potential clients and customers, from their competition.

At our college, along one edge of the property was a stone wall. On the outside there was a sign that read "Tyler School of Art." On the inside of the wall, someone had made a sign for everything out there that was *not* Tyler, and labeled it "The Real World". In this "real world", after college, you began to feel more of the pressure for perfection. Your work, in order to improve, required more time. Yet this flew in the face of the business aspect of what you did. In the end, it comes down to all of us, in any aspect of business, measuring some degree of average hourly pay for some level of work. Once again, art, unlike many other hourly or salary-based professions, blurs this concept. Does one spend (or invest) excess time perfecting a skill at a financial loss now in order to possibly gain back the financial reimbursement in the future? Often, yes. Works of art are frequently created out of love or struggle and the creative process often needs little more than that to justify its existence. But we are talking about a career here that balances creativity with business… your early career, through which you were looking at the viability of your talents providing a career, a purpose, a living for you. And in looking at your financial books in the basement after your death, I saw that you had a great first few years. I was honestly surprised and impressed at the business success that you achieved in your early career. Your career was working then.

There was one time period that I will always look back on and wonder about. You were living in the Society Hill Towers, living the "right-out-of-school-urban-existence". It was the "hot spot" of Philadelphia at the time, with sidewalk restaurants and some of the more historical buildings in the city. Suddenly, you severed any connection with friends and family. Calls were not answered, letters were not replied to. In looking back, I always felt that something happened, some emotional difficulty that you would never share with anyone your entire life. You said it was shame of seeing that your career was failing, but sorry, Kim, that's difficult to believe. About a year earlier, your fiancé broke off the engagement a month before your marriage. To be honest, at the time I didn't think he was right for you anyway... too much sports jock, too much party boy, not enough thought or emotion. Maybe it was simply when he came to the house after being out drinking and told me that he wasn't looking for an affair outside of your relationship but wouldn't argue if one came across his path. It was an odd thing to say to the younger brother of his fiancée, and a statement that forever positioned him in my mind as unworthy. Like you did with everything you touched, you had created a beautiful wedding experience, not huge but with all the details done just the way you wanted. It was a perfect custom dress, a small historical church, all the details that would make your wedding beautifully yours. But was this broken engagement the start of your process of self-destruction? Did it trigger a sleeping tendency?

After the first of what would be many discussions with Mom and Dad about your health, I suggested one course of action. Frustration and your choice to separate yourself from all friends and family was a motivating factor. I remember sneaking through the basement garage of your apartment, waiting for someone to come in, and getting in the elevator with him. You hadn't acknowledged my calls from the lobby so there was little else to do. I suppose it sounds a little intrusive or clinging, but after months of no response we were worried. Something was very wrong. High-rise apartment buildings tend to have a lot of glass so like some voyeur from a nearby street, I had seen you in your apartment and knew you were there. Knocking on your door, I talked to the faceless solid wood that returned nothing—no words, no request to leave you alone, nothing. When I tired of talking to myself, I abandoned the thought of talking with you and left, through the front door this time. I went back to relay the nothing that I had found. We knew that something serious was happening, and we knew that we could do nothing. This was a pattern that would define our relationship with you in one form or another for the rest of your life.

About ten months later, after many failed attempts to contact you, you showed a crack in the wall you were building. You asked to come out to the house and talk. I remember you appeared nervous and afraid that we wouldn't let you return to your apartment. Although we were extremely concerned, your fears seemed out of balance with our thoughts. There was never a thought of controlling you like that. But in another one of the many "what ifs" what if we did? I wish I had a better memory of that evening and of our discussion twenty-eight years ago. But from what I do recall, it was a discussion that revealed very little about a cause—no earth shattering reasons, no acknowledgement of understanding, just the beginning stages of your unnecessary shame of a difficult career.

Before and after your missing year, when I had hired you to do numerous illustration projects for me, I was very proud and happy to show people what came out of my concept and design work and my sister's illustration. Something much more important was happening; we were happy that you had reopened a dialogue with us, but something was different.

From that point it was a slow death in so many ways. You moved to a less expensive apartment and after Mom and Dad had to draw a financial line and stop lending you money for your apartment, you eventually moved back home with them. We saw the beginning of many projects that would never be finished, each one an honest and true belief on your part, that with enough work, it would be the "one" that could turn your career around. This became quite a challenge on our part, to dole out the proper support and encourage you in your life's goals, yet to direct you away from an ever-widening black hole of obsessive behavior. Over the years, you retreated from life. You shrank in every way possible, going from one of the most talented artists in your graduating class and an apartment in the "hot" part of town to a smaller apartment to our home that we grew up in to the basement of that home to the space around your drawing board to a hospital bed to a small box containing your ashes. It was a painful path to watch, and now we have to accept the fact that we didn't or couldn't make a difference in that path. "Didn't" or "couldn't"—each of those two words each carries with it a very different set of emotions.

A family develops habits of behavior built out of its repetitive experiences. It might be that one person always takes charge or that another always gets into financial trouble. Maybe someone always has to win arguments and another is always overly punctual. In the twenty-five years of dealing with a disease that until the very end you never accepted or admitted to having, you became the "broken one". We tried so hard not to define you that way to your face or even to ourselves. Viewing someone as any one thing can make it much harder for that person to change, even if she wants to. Our actions, whether driven by love or concern, can still slowly create an emotional box that someone is placed in, leaving her less and less of a way out. So we tried to deliver a balance of concern for the problems and reinforcement for your goals and work. It was a balance that had the wrong mix. Whether any "mix" could have worked, we will never know. Now, there is a strange emptiness, and not just from a missing sister and daughter. A focal point for our family is gone. We shared concern for you as a common goal, and many discussions revolved around your well-being. We discussed how to help, what to do, how to prepare for the future, what we could have or should have expected of you, anything that would help you and some things that might just help us cope. After twenty-five years of that focus, the need for our support is now gone. None of us ever wanted that task, but now that it's gone, there is a hollow feeling of missing a purpose that was there for so many years. And I wonder, *Did I miss out on the sister that I could have had because of your illness, or because, in my desire to help, I spent too much time looking at that illness and not enough time seeing you?*

TO REST

It's been about a year and a half since your death. I don't know if we've been avoiding the pain by not burying you yet, or if we wanted you near a little longer, but today, we are saying our final goodbye. I can't help thinking that a gravestone should be next to a husband's or at least next to a place reserved for him. Traditional thinking? Yes, but one can get that way with age or maybe just with moments like this. Or maybe it's just wishing that your life had turned out differently. It will be the three of us (Mom, Dad, and me) placing you in the grave next to our grandmother and grandfather. It's going to be a small event. I have broken up with Chanin, or more accurately, we have chosen to end our relationship, a pain that overrides almost everything right now, but her support won't be there. We have decided that this was time for just the family, as small as it is, to take this last trip with you alone.

I remember feeling a huge hole in the center of my chest when you died. I remember feeling that hole ever so slowly closing up as the months passed. I don't want that hole to open again. This is a challenging time for me. My fiancée and best friend is no longer by my side. Is this ability to be alone, playing with the thoughts of a solitary existence, all I can ask for? It makes me wonder about you. Was this what you gave in to as well? Was it what controlled your life? Is this little sliver of genetic material a common bond between us? Seeing what you went through in your life scares me more than anything I can think of. You had a point where your demons crept in and slowly took your ability to think productively and eventually took your life. I have seen many cases in the news or in reading history in which someone has changed into a dysfunctional bag of organs. Although I don't expect it, it would be naive to ignore any possibility of this in my life.

So with your burial, these fears returned… along with the emotions about you that I tried so hard to coax into the back seat of my mind. When we went to the cemetery, we carried the box with your ashes. It was the one they sold us at the funeral parlor. Early on, I remembered wanting to build something more special and more beautiful; this was not to be. I think in the past year, I began to try to focus on other aspects of life and to just experience that pain less.

I love the feeling of cemeteries. There is something calming and soulful about them. They represent a sense of permanency. You can walk through them and read names of so many people who lived, held jobs, married, had kids, laughed, and had some effect on the world in whatever little way they could. For many years, I have liked the idea of carving my own gravestone. Unfortunately, this flies in the face of a desire to be cremated in order to avoid taking up space for eternity. Sprinkling my ashes somewhere sounds perfect, maybe over a crystal blue ocean or the canyon lands of Utah.

The people at the cemetery office forgot to tell us to bring a specific piece of paperwork that somehow proves to the state that these ashes are actually you. So we sat for an hour or so waiting for them to contact the funeral home and get the forms faxed over. We talked, we waited, and we looked at the architecture that was considerably better than the funeral home. After the paperwork arrived, we drove to the burial site trying not to let the inconvenience of the paperwork process pull our emotional focus away from what we had to do. There are many relatives in this cemetery. Our great-grandparents, grandparents, great uncles and aunts all have their names in stone. As we pulled up in front of the site, they had the woven mesh walkway leading up to the grave and a little plastic pillar for us to place you on while we talked, read, and just thought. We had been through all the emotions before, and although we cried again, it was a short event. Dad read a passage from the Bible, we talked a little, held each other, and then I placed your ashes into the ground, holding my sister one last time. Mom and Dad went home, and I went back to work. It felt a little cold, a little distant, but we had been through so much emotion since your death that this seemed almost like a formality. But it was an important last process.

It was our last goodbye.

I had someone say to me once, "You should be Catholic with the guilt you feel." I always remembered that. It was a peculiar statement to hear. I escaped my youth without any strong religious attachment. We were raised Methodist, but at the age when we were given the decision to choose to continue with that faith, change faiths, or stop going to church all together, both you and I dropped out of the religious environment. I think artists generally look toward communities that accept and embrace individual thinking. Not all, but in my experience, many traditional religions seem to be trying to make more people fit their mold. This is, a comfortable and valuable place for some people, where a clear set of rules and behaviors to follow is wanted and where a supportive community of similar thinking can be found. I have developed a strong set of ethics but believe that this code of behavior can exist without the trappings and controls of a formal religion. I must admit though, I also have a strong curiosity about religion and like hearing about different peoples experiences with it. Maybe, like Groucho Marx said, "I never want to be part of a club that would have me as a member." Death does bring with it a certain focus on religion… or at least spirituality. Maybe that is simply the human condition, to try to make sense out of death, to understand where the people we love go, an attempt to still be with them. And I, like many before me, will struggle to gain an understanding of this.

AN UNFAIR COMPARISON

Time passes. The pain is less. I am beginning to think that I can step into making real choices in my life again. I feel a little ashamed that the impact of your death has been this extensive in my life, although to be honest, I really don't know the full extent of the impact. Maybe it's a result of simply a lack of practice with death or a reflection on the workings of my mind. Maybe it is what every other person goes through in these cases. Either way, it was and is an experience with little choice, and I have to believe that, in opening my heart to the pain, I am returning to being a feeling, caring human being.

A few days ago, I was watching a program on the history of the band Pink Floyd. Having grown up, or should I say, having my musically formative years in the '70s, I was raised on the wonderful complexities of progressive rock. I loved then, and still love now, the contrasts of pacing, the exploration of different musical styles, the general "why not, let's try it" attitude of that era. Like a lot of music, you can love the sound and never realize the lyrics or the meaning of the lyrics until years later. That was the case here. I loved the music of Pink Floyd, but until I had watched this program, I never understood the emotional struggle that drove the creation of many of their pieces. It was the early front man of the band (Syd Barrett) who was a charismatic, vibrant leader. Over time he slipped into a dysfunctional state and essentially became an emotionally absent friend and dysfunctional band member, a shell of a person that lived only as a body. The mind, the personality, the soul was all but gone. The pain of that loss resurfaced in much of the band's music after his departure in songs like "Shine on You Crazy Diamond" and "Wish You Were Here."

This simple TV program made me think about how people can "fall off the edge" and how the way that they fall effects those left behind. Okay, now here is the small print, the caveat, the reason for the chapter title: The pain of loss is different for everyone, and I don't mean for this to sound like I am saying that my pain is any more than anyone else's. A death from an accident, a death from a physical disease, a death from war all leave us with the pain and the questions of "why". But a death from self-chosen, destructive life styles, from essentially a long and damaging style of living seems to create a different pain. It may be the analogy of a quick death cutting like a sharp knife. The wound is just as deep but a sharp cut can heal faster. Watching the slow death of a person blind to the realities of their destruction rips and tears, leaving a jagged hole in our emotional health. Maybe it's simply the number of questions asked after a death that makes the difference. In a death resulting from an accident, the question is "Why were they in that accident?" In a death resulting from addiction, suicide, or in your case, anorexia, there are so many more questions. "Why did you have this illness?" "Is it genetic?" "Did we have any ability to affect it?" "If so how?" "When did it start?" "Was it one specific event that started it?" The pain from any loss is difficult. I just wonder if it's the number of unanswered questions that prolongs the healing process. And a mental illness leaves many unanswered questions behind.

INTROSPECTION

I have noticed that there seem to be two types of people in the world. How many times have you heard that as an opening line? But in this case, the ones I'm referring to either walk through their years with a basic philosophy that life is something that happens to them, as if they had little or no effect on the world around them, or they are people that experience life and look for what they can, learn from each situation. They look to see how they may have contributed to it. To be fair, I think that both options are valid at times and can be useful. "Everything in moderation," as the saying goes. Yet, and this may not be a surprise here, I mainly fall into the second of those two categories. As the years pass, I tend to look deeper and deeper for answers, and I have learned that "backing up" or trying to avoid painful thoughts, pretending that they're not important, is not an option. As a friend once said to me, "The only way around it is through it."

I have had no option but to look for the kernels of value that resulted from your death. If I were to describe these writings as one thing, I'd say that they are the search for that value. They are the ripping through the piles of intertwined emotional vines, some slowly dragging out and following long strands of a tangled mess with many branches to explore and an inability to find the "end". Other times, a grab and a pull result in a short, useless, and easily disposed of stick.

Through this I've asked a lot of questions, some leading to answers, some leading to more questions. I am inherently curious about everything, and I choose to believe this is a good trait. It helps me learn. But, the downside—there is always a downside somewhere—is that it can prevent me from standing on the solid foundation of firm assumptions and stepping forward into many of the advancements in life.

I've noticed in writing this, that creating something in an area that I am unfamiliar with, working in a media that, in my youth, I rejected in favor of the visual arts (English classes were merely something to put up with), I all too easily tended towards the very process that I accused you of embracing. It became a process of editing and re-editing, each time seeing new problems and making new adjustments. And there is a fear that I know you felt, "Will this ever be ready?"

Although my goal is quite the opposite, I am a little harder through this. My emotions run a little deeper below the surface of my being.

> The protective shell that I
> have built as protection from
> the pain of your death has
> prevented some of the fluid
> playfulness that allows for
> much of life's enjoyment.

There was a reason for this. It had its purpose. And now, my work—no, "work" is not the right word—my responsibility to myself is to lower that hard, cracked, old leather shield, to raise my arms not out of protection, but to embrace others and let others embrace me.

It has been a path through a difficult event and one that I have tried to record in the best way that I could, at times throwing words on a page like Jackson Pollack's paint, not knowing what patterns would arise but believing that there was value somewhere in the process, and at times, pausing over a word, frustrated with my inability to create the right message. In the end, it is what it is: raw, painful, silly, primitive, all exactly what it has to be.

Is this important? To some: maybe, to others: no. Like anything in life, we see, we explore, we experience, and we pick out the value for each of us and discard the rest. The original purpose in writing this was personal; it was to help me deal with the pain of your death and to record an experience that I didn't want to forget. It became a place for me to learn and heal. There are endless groups with the goal of gathering people with similar experiences in order to share their similar difficulties and to learn how to handle them. I suspect many of them serve a very valuable purpose and function as an island for those troubled by any number of challenges. I have heard from quite a few people that their experiences, although focused on other specific concerns, like alcoholism or drug abuse, were quickly superseded by a much larger understanding of life's personal issues. It can be a growth that goes way beyond a substance addiction or a single distorted way of thinking. Why does it take tragedy to learn the things that should be part of our core education from an early age?

I was worried when I gave a draft of this to Mom and Dad. Would it be too personal? Would it bring them back to a pain that they didn't want to feel again? Would it be a story that they would rather keep as our personal possession? As their only living child, I have to and want to respect their opinions. You were their child. You were their little girl who grew through the innocence of your adolescence through the optimism of early adulthood into a challenge that was simply too powerful to control. When the phone rang, through tears, they both voiced their appreciation for seeing our emotional path in writing, and they said that they hoped it would be published. It was an approval on a personal and public level, and it eased my concerns.

It's an awkward feeling, opening one's ribs to show the heart, with all its fears and concerns, as well as its strengths and successes. And on this topic, who am I to choose to reveal your difficulties. In many ways, it would be easier to finish this writing and store it away in some drawer never to see the public eye. There would be no concerns of outside opinion. No questions of, "Did I say it clearly enough?" no wondering if this is what you would have wanted... or maybe *now* want. I have to think, or maybe I have chosen to think, that death frees one of all the silly earthly concerns. You did, after all, want to donate your body in order to help someone else. I too, acknowledge that, as I get older, there is a growing drive to make a positive difference in the world. Maybe this is simply seeing my mortality over some distant horizon. Maybe it is actually a sign of deeper learning and an understanding of one's priorities. It's hard to know if we are actually making a difference in the world. Some actions seem so little, like picking up an old discarded can when walking in some vacant woods. Does it really matter? I don't know, but it's my choice to do it anyway.

This book too will be another choice, and I believe that you support me in this. There is value in writing it on a personal level for me. But like many expressions, is that proof of value for others? Will it "make a difference?" That is for others to determine, who through random chance, or deliberate searching find their way into these pages.

THE END

It's a rainy Saturday in October. Warm enough to have the doors of the house open, letting the sound of the rain sweep through the house. It creates a backdrop, not unlike the hypnotic music of the ocean that I've always loved.

As I have written this, especially as I near the end of these words, I have wondered, what can be learned from all this, how can a book like this (I call it a book now because I'm beginning to think that it just might be one) be "wrapped up" in some nice little uplifting package? How do I complete these pages of pain with a degree of hope? I don't think I can... or should. This is a simple delivery of a tragic experience and of the emotional path leading up to, during, and after a death. But in the name of "misery loves company" or just the fact that there is comfort in knowing others have similar experiences, I have to wonder, are similar challenges being met by someone else with an anorexic loved one, or maybe a family's struggle with addiction, or simply people who have just lost someone. I really can't know.

I do know that writing this, although difficult, has been the best possible path through my own varied and confusing emotions. I can sit here and think, *we failed* or *you failed* or *the health industry failed* or *the disease was greater than anyone could control.* All these statements may have a greater or lesser degree of truth. That degree of truth for each may even change from one day to the next as I drift from a memory of the playful and fun time we had as kids to a memory of you at your last slow and labored breath. You were in my life not only as a focus of concern, not only as the one that needed help so desperately, but as someone who laughed and loved and cared deeply about others. You were my "big" sister who first introduced me to the music of our youth. You were (and maybe still are) brilliant and creative, and you taught me so many things about how to look at or think about art, how to maintain a focus on goals, how to try to keep a positive attitude in times of apparent failure. Most of all, you were you, with all the complexities (maybe more than most) that make people different and amazing in their own way.

It's difficult to step back and simply say that your life was how you "had" to live and that it was your choice and we should respect that. It may be what we have to do to separate ourselves from the pain but after so many years of trying to help, we have to now learn how to abandon the thinking of a possible solution and accept that it was beyond our ability. We have to shift the cause of your death from your choices to the disease that no one could control. We have to remember, however difficult, that after so many years of being in the role of advisor, therapist, brother and parent, that you were not then and are not now defined by your illness. It was something you just had, like a bad back, allergies or flat feet. And in this case, the thing you "just had" killed you.

I have walked through this experience with you to the best of my ability. At times I was furious with the stubborn woman that refused help, angry at the pain you unintentionally handed to your family. But as I have written this, as I have given myself the time to explore the different choices you made. I am slowly learning to separate the pain from the love, the anger from understanding, and maybe most importantly, your self-destructive actions from the person that you really were, and in many ways still are. The definition of Kim in my mind is shifting from the hurt and fragile woman that I saw for so many years to a person that had the strength and determination to strive for what she wanted. Not for society. Not for logic. Not for the simple need to survive in this world, but for your own personal desires. You had your struggles, but the true definition, the true understanding of who you were, of who you are, goes so far beyond that. There is a beauty to that person. There is a joyful and wondrous soul underneath the years of pain. There is a lesson in that for me. You were not intended to be here in our time for any longer than you were. Many times I've heard this said and viewed it as a cliché, as a cute little spiritual statement that automatically comes out when there is no other way to find logic or reason. But I have to try to believe that your time here was never intended to be in the same time frame as that of your family. You lived and struggled, and in the purity of your belief, you crashed against the world that you so wanted to be different... and maybe it was also a world that wanted you to be different. On a basic physiological level, yes you had an illness that took your life, a complex illness, a difficult one, and one that challenged the boundaries between physiological and emotional answers. But on a human and personal level you had a strength that I truly admire, whether it be in continuing to try, to reach for goal after goal after goal, with all your physical and emotional challenges, or the intense focus on what you wanted even when those around you were desperately trying to teach you another way... you were you.

With the passing of years the Kim with the illness fades. The struggle, the pain and the sorrow of watching your self-destruction lessens. The Kim who I knew to be there all along is emerging. The pain of a loss often brings with it a ride through new and uncomfortable emotions. But that ride brings us to a new place… a place where we can see over the fog of struggle, beyond the pain of confrontation, and maybe past the loneliness of death, to the beauty of a life.

And after it all, after the sorrow and the questions, after the pain and the desire to use this experience to help some unknown someone out of their personal prison, I find that I am still here. I am still in this life, living, working, navigating my own challenges, some with success, and some failures. Attempting to make each day a little better, attempting to *be* a little better. This is my path; to spend the time I have to the best of my ability. I will continue to miss you and to honor your life. And as time passes, I find that I am slowly returning to honoring mine.

GONE FROM MY SIGHT

I am standing upon the seashore. A ship at my side spreads her white sails in the morning breeze and starts for the blue ocean.

She is an object of beauty and strength and I stand and watch her until at last she hangs like a white cloud just where the sea and sky come down to mingle with each other.

Then someone at my side says, " There, she's gone." Gone where? Gone from my sight, that is all. She is just as large in the mast and hull and spar as she was when she left my side, and just as able to bear her load of living freight to the place of destination.

Her diminished size is in me, not in her. And just at that moment someone at my side says,"There she is gone." there are other eyes watching her coming and other voices ready to take up the glad shout: "Here she comes!"

Dying is like that. The journey continues. God is our Pilot, and will see us safely to that farther shore.

Anonymous

TO KIM,

I wish you had lived; yet I know that the strength of your illness was beyond your control… and anyone's ability. I wish you could have had a happy and fulfilling life. I will miss the *you* that you let out from time to time and I know this woman existed under the painful layers of the disorder, and I will miss the relationship with the sister and the best friend that I wished for us. I will think of you without ever losing the feeling of sadness and I will try to believe (however convenient of a philosophy it is) that you are in a better place exploring your perfect creativity. I wish to live my life with the memory of you firmly in my heart, but not defining my life. And at some time in the future, some place where we might meet again, I wish to be able to talk to you about all of this and understand it better.

I love you,

Bill

It's been a little over five years since my sister's passing. For the sake of completing the story and my experience (to date) it seems appropriate to write a little about what has happened in my life in more recent years.

In the numerous times reading through this, even this many years after the original event of my sister's passing I see the struggle to understand and a process of questioning almost everything. Yes, this is my nature. And like any habit, I see both it's benefits and liabilities.

Chanin and I did return to a committed relationship. We were married a year and a half ago and bought a cute little Victorian house in Doylestown PA. We love working on the house and getting involved in various social, creative and business activities. About six months after our marriage, Chanin's mother passed away from cancer. It was and is a new experience with all the difficulties that one would expect. It also provided some unexpected joys of new friendships that indirectly resulted from her passing. We sprinkled her ashes in the crystal blue water in the Bahamas while on a friends sail boat in 2010. It was a beautiful day.

I am still running my design and marketing firm and enjoy making a difference in the success of my client's businesses.

As we travel through life and see years add up behind us, our perspective changes with each new experience. Each joy, each sorrow widens our understanding. They make us a little more patient, give us the understanding to direct our lives a little better, help us to prioritize more effectively and show us the ever more detailed instruction book for our lives. To all those experiences... thank you.